CONTACT
PHOTOGRAPHERS

7TH EDITION

ISBN NO 1 870458 17 6

Contact
Photographers
Annual

Publishers
Nicholas Gould
Barry O'Dwyer

Published by
Elfande Art Publishing
Unit 39
Bookham Industrial Park
Church Road
Bookham Surrey
KT23 3EU

Telephone 0372 459559
Telefax 0372 459699

Cover Photography by
Bob Carlos Clarke

Photography this spread
by Tony Bowran one of the
Gold Award winners in this years
Association Of Photographers
awards

Printed in Singapore
by Toppan Printing Co. Ltd

Typesetting by
John Hobson

Production Director
Nicholas Gould

Sales Executive
Juliette Kellar

Administration
Jo Rennison

Book design &
Art direction by
Barry O'Dwyer

This years front cover by **Bob Carlos Clarke** is one of twelve powerful images specially created for the **PowerGen 1991 Calendar**. The calendar was conceived and produced by McCann-Erickson (Solihull). Its creative rationale was given as follows:

'The theme for the PowerGen 1991 Calendar is based on the various "powers" which shape and change all our lives.

We therefore carefully position PowerGen as an intellectually-aware energy producer which acknowledges that imagination and inspiration, for instance, are just as forceful as the power of electricity itself.

The creative platform for the calendar makes use of quotations by famous "thinkers" to form the basis of the 12 months, each quotation representing a different power, which is qualified and developed by the particular image.

As with any calendar, these images are crucial in communicating the overall message. To be effective, each image should be capable of continually impressing the onlooker, exciting anyone who sees it for the first time and, of course, reinforcing the PowerGen branding.

To achieve these criteria, each image had to be an authoritative work of art, not just a contrived photograph supporting the particular proposition.

It was therefore easy to choose a photographer; Bob Carlos Clarke is one of the most imaginative contemporary photographers and is best-known for his strong, dramatic shots.

With all twelve quotations chosen, it was important to decide upon a theme for the photography. In this case, it is impact and simplicity, which together produce such a distinctive style for the PowerGen 1991 calendar. '

Bob Carlos Clarke was born in Ireland in 1950. Originally trained as a journalist and graphic designer but developed an interest in photography at the West Sussex College of Art in 1969. He continued his studies at The London College of Printing and later at The Royal College of Art.

Bob Carlos Clarke has had four books published to date: The Illustrated Delta of Venus (1979), Obsession (1981), The Dark Summer (1985) and White Heat (1990).

He is represented by Hamiltons Gallery in London and his photographs are exhibited and collected worldwide. He is well known for his portraits of the rich and famous as well as many leading advertising campaigns including Smirnoff, Levis, Pirelli, Vladivar, Volkswagen, Fiat, Panasonic and Agfa.

Bob Carlos Clarke is currently completing work on a new book of photographs scheduled for publication later this year.

POWERGEN CALENDAR
CONCEIVED AND PRODUCED BY
McCANN-ERICKSON (SOLIHULL)
CREATIVE DIRECTOR GRAHAM SMITH
ART DIRECTION GRAHAM SMITH
COPYWRITING DENIS O'KEEFFE
DESIGN JOHN JENKINSON
TYPOGRAPHY MARK BLACKBURN

BENSON & HEDGES GOLD AWARDS 1990

In the throes of judging the photographic entries in the 1990 Benson and Hedges Gold Awards were (pictured left to right): Mark Porter, art director of Direction and Campaign magazines; Paul Briginshaw, senior art director at Collett Dickenson Pearce and Partners; Eamonn McCabe, picture editor of the Guardian; Angus Woolhouse from Benson and Hedges; and Jay Myrdal, photographer and past chairman of the Association of Photographers.

The five judges had the challenging task of assessing some 478 professional and student photographs, all submitted as interpretations of the one-word brief "Magic". From the entries the judges were looking to identify three professional award winners, one student award winner, and ten highly commended winners.

The panel was photographed by Mike Laye, visualised by Roger Swanborough & assembled by Roger Singer.

Born 1967. Emma is studying for a MA in photography at the Royal College of Art. Her photograph interprets Magic as the illusion of a false reality.

❝ The theme "Magic" in the Benson and Hedges Gold Awards struck me immediately as an ideal opportunity to compete. Competitions so often deal with themes outside of my interests, and this title ran parallel to the ideas that constantly run throughout my work, that is, the play of visual illusion.

My primary interest in the Photographic image is in it's illusion of a visual "truth". I am excited by the possible exploitations of this deception, the fact that the unreal can be given some substance simply because of the "window on the world" reputation that parasitically clings to it's photographic host.

The piece I entered for the competition, "Spinning Around The Moon", was shown as a 12 x 16 Cibachrome in the exhibition, although the original piece is a 7 x 3 ft triptych printed onto canvas and tinted with oils. It is important to me that this is seen as the original, as the texture and image surface are very important to the overall quality of all my work.

Even though, sadly, this piece was not shown in it's original form I was not disappointed by the show. The whole event was executed with a professionalism, preceded by a huge advertising campaign that surprised me. Also as a result of being involved in this award I received interest from a few galleries and agencys, so I found the competition valuable in that respect. As a student, money is always an incentive to make attempts at competitions such as this one, and as the results were announced all I could feel was an intense but wonderful shock. ❞ **Emma Parker**

❛ Certain places have an indefinable "Magic" quality about them. I tried to capture on film the feeling that I have experienced in places where man has left his mark, the Pyramids, Roman ruins and abandoned quarries all have this quality.

A little help from seven or eight portable flash packs, a long wait for the light and a great printer (Keith Taylor) and I

I think that awards are great (I would, wouldn't I!). I've been lucky to have won one or two. It's unfortunate that there is only one "GOLD". I believe that the selection for inclusion in the exhibition is the most important thing. Taking photographs which remain unseen is a little pointless. People should put themselves on the line and enter.

I have been busy for quite a while, but I hope that the exposure will prompt a few Designers and Art Directors to ask to see the book. Hopefully I might get a few commissions, but I don't think that there is much of a call for a photographer of Burial Chambers! *Lorentz Gullachsen*

'When I thought of magic I remembered sitting with my dad watching Tommy Cooper on television. I remember his helpless expression, he always looked so nervous and of course his fez. That was my motivation for the shot and it seemed right to have a calm static picture in view of his death.

I was pleased to win second prize, mainly because of the money. It will pay for the hire of the dove along with other costs and it will also help finance other test shots as this is part of a series.

Often with competitions people slate the results as being boring or not fulfilling the brief or that the standards are very poor. While this is sometimes true I still believe that they are worthwhile because it allows exposure to non commercial work and gives people a chance to earn money from something that may be a personal project. Perhaps if the people that slate the awards entered better or more appropriate work the standards would improve, this would surely help photography as a whole. I would like to see more recognition for fine art photographers and more acceptance of this kind of work in a commercial environment as I believe the two can cross over and that competitions can be a place where this can happen.

Good pictures and good results in awards can lead to work but its not automatically so. Often I think that the right people just don't see the results. However, I have had work as a result of publications before.' **Adrian Burke**

'MAGIC' BY ADRIAN BURKE

KEN GRIFFITHS won a Gold and the award for
'best of show'.

Every year the Association strives to improve the fairness and integrity of the judging, and this year was no exception, major changes were introduced; where previously, no entry had been seen by more than six judges, this year every picture was seen by no fewer than nineteen! The jury was composed of people with unquestioned experience in the world of media photography — as photographers or art directors. A truly distinguished panel.

Over 2,300 images were submitted and the judges were given two whole days in which to make their choices. The first day's consensus eliminated some two thirds of the total entry. The second day further reduced the balance, and the highest scoring pictures were seen for a third time to consider their viability for Gold and Silvers.

The Presentation of the Eighth Awards took place on 12th February 1991, at the Barbican Hall the Award winners were announced. The exhibition was then on show at the Association Gallery, 9-10 Domingo Street EC1 for one month from 18th February, before it commenced its tour to major photographic venues throughout the UK and Europe.

The Eighth Awards Book, will be available from 13th February.

For further information on the Awards, the tour, press prints or if you would like to reserve a review copy of the Awards Book, please contact Valerie Lawton on 071-608 1441.

BRANKA JUKIC — Gold award

ANTONIA DEUTSCH — Gold award

TONY BOWRAN — Gold award

Judging for the Eighth Awards took place over tow days in October, at Eagle Wharf Studios in London N1. There were nineteen judges this year:

Paul Briginshaw - CDP
Joanna Dickerson - J Walter Thompson
Neil Godfrey - CDP
John Horton - Abbott Mead Vickers/SMS
Zelda Malan - Saatchi & Saatchi
Alan Waldie - Lowe Howard Spink

Photographers:
Gary Bryan
Adrian Flowers
Lorentz Gullachsen
Andreas Heumann
Sandra Lousada
Tim O'Sullivan
Bob Miller

Directors:
Bob Cramp
Julian Cottrell
Tony May

Mike Dempsey - Carroll Dempsey Thirkell
Robert Valentine - Habitat
Mark Whitaker - GQ Magazine

Michael Westmoreland FBIPP FRPS has been described as 'Britains foremost panorama photographer' * He has been experimenting with panoramic images and equipment since the early 1970's and was given the RICHARD FARRAND AWARD (1984) in this connection. This is presented jointly by the British Institute of Professional Photography and the Royal Photographic Society for technical distinction in Applied Photography. He has received several other awards, has exhibited widely in various prestigious locations, has work in many public and private collections and received numerous commissions.
* From the book 'Panoramania', produced for the exhibition of that title at the Barbican, London 1988.

❛ Photographers the world over are constantly striving for fractional improvements in the information content of their images. Manufacturers and designers devote their working lives to satisfying that hunger: hence the never-ending quest for sharper lenses, better resolution, finer grain, improved contrast. Such is the present sophistication of the technology that gains in these areas which are quite undiscernible to the non-photographer become the major sensation at Photokina. One way of making a spectacular escape from these cramping confines is to eschew conventional binocular vision altogether, and use a panoramic camera, which in certain embodiments permits the totality of a complete 360 degrees.

What is a panoramic camera? As far as I am concerned as a serious operator, there is only one type which is of any real use to me, and that is the totally rotating/ moving film/slit-scan/ 360- degree design. There are simpler cameras which employ a curved film plane and swinging-lens, but they are usually restricted to 140 degrees and interchangeable lenses and lens movements are out of the question. There is a further category often erroneously labelled 'panoramic' which should more properly be called 'panoramic format': these commonly employ a rollfilm body with extended film aperture and wide-angle lens covering a maximum 105 degrees. Exactly the same results can be obtained with a large format camera.

When I got interested in panoramic images all those years ago there was absolutely nothing on the market which would do the kind of result I was after. It was necessary to buy museum equipment and modify it in various ways for modern lens and film technology: it was also necessary to devise all kinds of one-off methodologies for processing, printing and translation for reproduction. The cameras were cumbersome but had one absolutely priceless asset which has never since been incorporated into a panoramic camera design: an enormously — flexible bellows which permits a great range of lenses and lens movements. One of my cameras can be adapted to take lenses between 24 inch and 2¼ inch focal length. Only when you get down to the business of trying to take panoramas in a wide variety of locations does this kind of facility really become appreciated: the turning camera imposes an extremely limited choice of stance, so more choice of lenses and movements on offer must considerably increase the chances of making a more useful photograph. There are now well-made but very expensive 360-degree cameras available but these mostly have non-interchangeable lenses of short-focal length. Photographers tend to hire them to play about with and the results are often consequently unimpressive.

All this leads to the question which should be carefully pondered by the picture-user; do you want a panoramic-format image purely for its aesthetic qualities, or do you need true panoramic subject coverage beyond the limits of the 105-degree wide-angle lens, without resorting to the obvious distortions of fish-eyes and other optical gizmos? (contrary to popular notions, slit-scan images do not distort: laying them out flat instead of wrapping them around you shows the curvilinear effect of true perspective). All the pictures I have shown in *Contact* illustrate the information content within 140-360 degree subjects: I leave it to the viewer to decide whether they have their own aesthetic. The point is that the user is offered a totality and is then free to crop down to whatever he likes: with the more limited offerings of other sorts of cameras he doesn't know what he might have missed.

TECHNICAL AND SUBJECT POSSIBILITIES

What most people initially expect of a panoramic camera is that it can make a grand city or landscape panorama in the heroic tradition. That is what the Edwardian monster illustrated here, with its enormous film rolls and information gathering potential, was built to do. What is not generally realised is that many of the most obvious subjects of this kind have all the essential drama contained within a few degrees around the horizon level. Hence the great value of long-focus lenses and the shortcomings of many modern cameras in this respect.

A different possibility is that the width of pan may be purposefully used to demonstrate spatial relationships within the shot: for example, a hotel brochure might benefit from a turning shot within a living space which spanned a series of open doors giving glimpses of kitchen, bathroom, bedroom and balcony.

The actual time it takes to make the exposure may be used to advantage for certain effects. Everybody remembers the school group photograph and the hoary old stories about people appearing on both ends. Subjects temporarily out of scan may move any number of times within the photograph if the length of film permits. On the other hand, the camera may remain static during exposure, with moving film and moving subject brought into co-ordination. Thus are made periphery shots of people and objects on turntables which finish up looking something like a bearskin rug, and extraordinary images of moving subjects such as traffic or athletes.

The giant panorama of London spans 270 degrees. It was originated on a piece of aerofilm colour transparency measuring 7 ½ feet by 9 ½ inches, which is 500 times the area of a 35mm frame. The film was housed in a 70-year-old modified panoramic camera, using a 24" long distance lens. Similiar equipment using an extreme wide-angle 4½ inch lens coped with the tightly-enclosed 360-degree surroundings of Piccadilly Circus shown on Page 52/53. In complete contrast, the other picture is a vertical panorama covering a 180-degree cathedral roofscape made on a piece of 35mm film exposed in a tiny specially-built interchangeable-lens camera.

These pictues illustrate something of the versatility which is possible if the panoramic photographer is willing to go beyond the limits of conventionally-available equipment.
See pages 52/53 for further illustrations.

USAGE POSSIBILITIES

Photo-decor: A growing field for architects and interior designers. I have sold to all manner of customers, public and private, for use in hospitals, clinics, offices, schools and public spaces of all kinds. I have a great advantage here: almost certainly alone among photographers I originate on large aerofilm

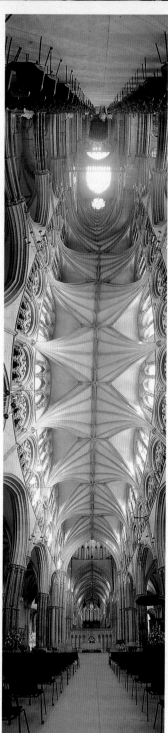

transparency, and this gives unique access to the near-archival Cibachrome derivations which are a great selling-point for the long-term user.

Information and Display: Panoramas with captions make superb explanatory panels for tourist spots, nature trails etc. I made two such for the Walkways vantage point high on Tower Bridge. New encapsulation techniques can provide ultra long-life UV and vandal-proof protection for externally-used Cibas.

Books and printed matter: I have had some impressive use made of my material across several pages and in foldouts. There is great scope for bookjackets, concertina-brochures and the like.

Advertising: Long narrow spaces abound everywhere, often unused, often split up into smaller rectangles. My special eye constantly notices sides of buses, eye-level panels in Tube trains, corridors of all kinds. It is encouraging that some available ad panels are now moving away from the conventionally-proportioned-rectangle: the illustration I did for Schroders bank was specially shot to fit an existing 25 by 5 foot backlit panel at the London City Airport (page 52).

Interior Designers: are increasingly concerned with even larger spaces: malls, amphitheatres, terminals, superstores, hotels etc.
Exhibition Designers with giant conventions:
Architects needing progression shots on all manner of sites. All of these can make use of the scanning photograph to convey comprehensive visual information to their clients providing they are conversant with the available possibilities.

Picture-users are often also designers, and designers are trained to find solutions for problems. On the other hand, scientists often provide solutions and wait for problems to turn up; for example the laser quietly languished for some years after it was invented. The panoramic image perhaps bridges both categories: it was once described to me by a bigwig at Kodak as a 'sleeping giant of the photographic domain'. To be fully exploited it needs some lateral thinking by people on the lookout for something different. If you are reading this book the chances are that you might fit into this category.
(MY details and further illustrations are on pages 52-53). ❞

PHOTOGRAPHERS INDEX

PETE GARDNER

5 Charterhouse Works
Eltringham Street
London SW18 1TD
Tel: 081-871 3975

DESMOND BURDON v

Studio 4
38 St. Oswalds Place
SE11
Tel: 071-582 0559
Fax: 071-582 4528

STUDIO

Represented in London by Nicola Crawford
Tel: 071-582 0559   Fax: 071-582 4528
Represented in Milan by Vitoria Speziali
Tel: 498 0426   Fax: 481 93788
Represented in Dusseldorf by Milena Najdanovic
Tel: 890 3444   Fax: 890 3999
Represented in Los Angeles by SFIDA
Tel: 965 1984   Fax: 965 8623
Represented in New York by Susan Miller
Tel: 905 8400   Fax: 427 7777

MICHAEL DUNNING

Contact: Sara Wheeler

18 West Central Street
Covent Garden
London WC1A 1JJ
Tel: 071-836 3110
Fax: 071-240 3992

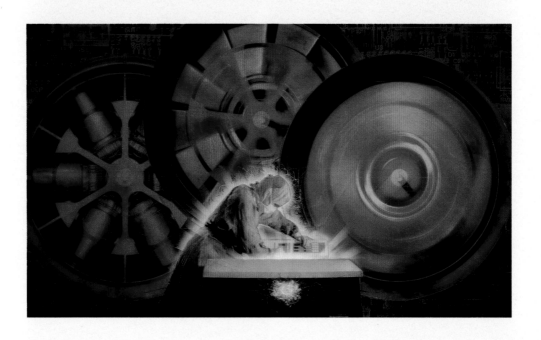

JEAN — LOUIS BATT

Colour Montage
Business
People

167 Trellick Tower
Golborne Road
London W10 5UT
Tel: 081 - 968 4948
Fax: 081 - 968 4948

Unitech —Agency: Micheal Peters & Partners

Business Today

SIMON WILLIAMS
PHOTOGRAPHY

Contact: Simon Williams

Studio 1
40 Rosemary Drive
Redbridge
London IG4 5JD
Tel: 081-551 8934

26

XING ART PRODUCTIONS GmbH

Contact: Hugo Mayer-Norten, C.C.

Kirchenstr. 54 B
D - 8000 München 80
Tel: 089/ 448 28 34
Fax: 089/ 48 68 89

XING Art Productions GmbH. Creative action for satisfaction.
Presents photographers and illustrators.

VORMWALD

GEISSLER

COIGNY

H.M. NORTEN

MATTHEW ANTROBUS

Photography
Inside
Outside
Worldwide

Unit 406
31 Clerkenwell Close
London EC1R 0AT
Tel: 071-251 2837

PETER HINCE v

Shaftesbury House
13/14 Hoxton Market
Coronet Street
London N1 6HG
Tel: 071-729 6727
Fax: 071-739 2321

Paris
Represented by Cosmos
Tel: 33 (1) 45 06 18 80

People, Fashion/Beauty, Lifestyle.
Studio or location shots with life and movement.
Full production facilities.
Extensive international experience.
Clients include:
Barclaycard, Boots, BMW, British Airways,
British Telecom, Canon, Crookes Healthcare, Dolcis,
Dunlop/Slazenger, Fuji, Gillette, House of Fraser,
Ralph Lauren, Prudential Insurance, Renault, Janet Reger,
ROC Cosmetics, Titleist Golf Wear, Wella, Wolsey.

PATRICK COCKLIN

Area of expertise:

Shoots most still life situations, with an emphasis on model making and special effects.

14a Hesper Mews
London SW5
Tel: 071-373 7850

KIM WILLIAMS

Specialising in:
Corporate Identity, Travel, Landscapes, Locations, and People.

Tel: 071-732 3241
Pager: 081-884 3344 Code A321

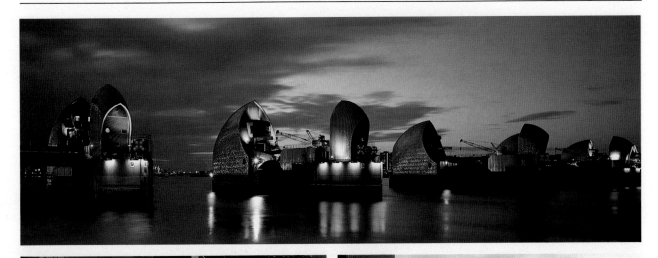

STUNNING CORPORATE PHOTOGRAPHY

Contact: Steve Dunning

273 Chiswick Village
London
W4 3DF
Tel: 081-995 2259

Our speciality is location photography under difficult conditions. We make the best of grotty factories, clapped-out machines and dark offices, to get great pictures for company advertising, annual reports and brochures. Whether a week under the Arabian sun, a day in the factory — or ten minutes between board meetings, we have the experience and techniques to come away with something, well, Stunning!
Recent clients include: AST Computers, Grampian TV, Iveco Ford, Kodak, Liberty, London & Edinburgh Trust, Management Computing, Miele, Sanderson, Securiguard Plc, Siemens UK. & Thorn EMI.

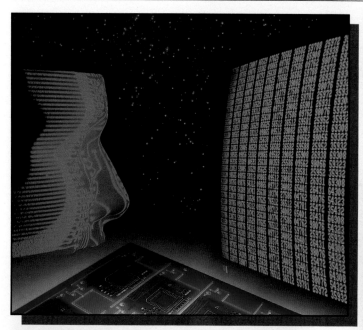

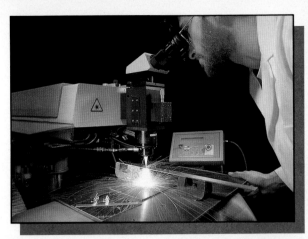

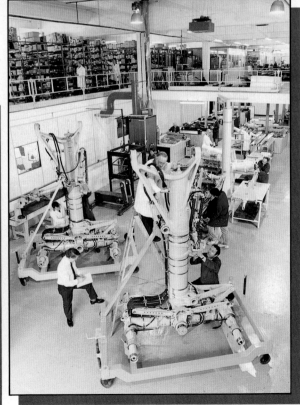

TONY HUTCHINGS

44 Earlham Street
Covent Garden
London WC2H 9LA
Tel: 071-379 6397

Agent Sylvia Schroer
Tel: 071-498 3211

PETER J MILLARD v

Studio 5
Scampston Mews
London W10 6HX
Tel: 081-968 1377
Fax: 081-968 0104
Mobile: 0831 465240

Also available in colour.

29 Waterside
44-48 Wharf Road
London N1 7SH
Tel: 071-253 0157
Fax: 071-253 0168

Agent in Paris: MAEVE
Tel: 42 85 34 87

44 **BRIAN PHIPPS** v

Peregrine House
Enborne Street
Enborne
Newbury
Berkshire RG14 6RP
Tel: 0635 42585
Fax: 0635 528775
Mobile: 0836 289377

46 **COLIN MOLYNEUX**

Contact: Helen or Stephanie

Tel: 0291 625013
Mobile: 0836 216909
Fax: 0291 627215

Andrew and Colin work both as a team and
independently for a wide variety of international clients.
We specialise in photography for annual reports,
location advertising, corporate brochures and A/VS.
For creative work without the hassle call to see
our portfolio.
For stock images call THE IMAGE BANK offices
worldwide or call Helen on 0291 625013

Pictures courtesy South West Electricity, Olympia & York
Canada, T&N USA and Peat Marwick McLintock.

CHRIS HONEYWELL

33 Marston Street
Oxford OX4 1JU
England
Tel: (0865) 246311
   (0865) 793278 (Studio)
Message Pager: 0399 1133
Pager no. 740237

Specialising in:
Corporate and Industrial Photography at home
and abroad.

Client:
Skerman Fabrications Ltd
162 Windmill Road West
Sunbury on Thames
Middlesex TW16 7HB

TONY ROBINS

Clerkenwell Chambers
82-84 Clerkenwell Road
London EC1M 5RJ
Tel: 071-251 0097/0102

Food
Still Life
Personalities
Location

Specialist Advertising Area:
Working closely with a fine artist I can incorporate
client's products into fine art painted backgrounds in the
style of any artist. For examples of this work and any
of the above subjects please contact Joy Sibbritt
on 071-251 0097.

STRUAN WALLACE v

Contact: Photographers agent
Sandie 081-861 4383

The Studio
16 Gibraltar Walk
London E2
Tel: 071-739 4406
Fax: 071-739 8784

Area of expertise: Food, Drink & Still-Lifes
Major clients include: Sainsburys, Waitrose, ASDA, Carling Black Label, Courvoisier, Johny Walker, Fortnum & Mason, House of Fraser, various books & magazine publications.

Many thanks to Sara Maxwell for food styling the shot appearing below.

LEONARDO FERRANTE

75 Esmond Road
London
W4 1JE
Tel: 081-994 1203

I specialise in Industrial photography, Company reports, architectural and abstracts. I have my own library of stock photographs available.

52

MICHAEL
WESTMORELAND v

358 Victoria Park Road
Leicester LE2 IXF
England
Tel: 0533-705828

Specialist panoramic location photographer of many
years experience, offering unique variety of services.
Film formats from 35mm by 70mm to 10 inch by 10 feet.
See page 12-13 for further details.

Malta harbourfront (section) 190 degrees from 4 inches by 108 inches tran.

Northamptonshire landscape 180 degree. 4$\frac{1}{2}$ inches by 36 inches tran.

Harringworth Viaduct 270 degrees. 9$\frac{1}{2}$ inches by 90 inches (section).

Bank of England 270 degrees, 3$\frac{1}{2}$ inches by 15 inches negative.

Schroders
Take Another View

Hong Kong from Hilton hotel. 200 degrees 6 inches by 30 inches tran.

Piccadilly Circus 360 degrees. 8 inches by 32 inches tran.

Kloster Port 4A
DK/8000
Arhus C
Denmark
Tel: +45 8619 16 74

TONY LATHAM

Space Studios
Symes Mews
37 Camden High Street
London NW1 7JE
Tel: 071-251 4386
Mobile: 0831 473954

During the last 10 years I have built up a considerable knowledge of people, places and locations.

My work has taken me all over the U.K., Europe and the world, with commissions from leading advertising, design and editorial clients.

I have photographed many leading figures and personalities, Sir Roy Strong, Peter Gabriel, and Joanna Lumley being some of the most recent.

Consequently, this has enabled me to build a unique collection of Library transparencies which are available for stock use.

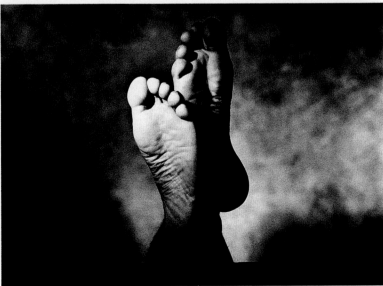

CLIVE SAWYER

Woodland Cottage
2 Mount Close
Pound Hill
Crawley
Sussex RH10 7EF
Tel: 0293 885588
Mobile: 0831 110085
Fax: 0293 885588

A photographer with wide experience shooting on location, both in the U.K. and abroad.
Continually updated stock photography taken for a leading colour library, Pictures (Tel: 071-497 2034, see page178), includes subjects on lifestyle, architecture, industry, commerce as well as some unique views of London.

IAIN GRAHAM

147 Nelson Road
Whitton
Middlesex TW2 7BB
Tel: 081-894 3202
or Message Pager: 081-840 7000
Code 0781793

Area of Speciality:
Corporate
People
Location
Architecture
Interiors

58　**RON DAVIES**

22a South Road
Waterloo
Liverpool L22 5PQ
Tel: 051-928 7447
Mobile: 0860 434144

Studio based, but works mostly on location, for advertising, annual reports and brochures. Experienced in Aerials, Editorial, Exteriors and Interiors, Industry, Landscapes, People, Public Relations and Pictorial Images.

Atmospheric stock shots of local scenes.

Clients include: National Museums on Merseyside, NatWest, Mecca Leisure, Merseyside Tourism Board, Radio City, Royal Life, Rumbelows and United Biscuits.

GRANT C SMITH

International Building Press
Photographer of the Year 1990.

145 Mildenhall Road
London E5 ORY
Tel: 081-985 1101

WILKINSON
ROBERT WILKINSON PHOTOGRAPHY

39 Villiers Avenue
Surbiton
Surrey KT5 8BB
Tel: 081-390 2237
Mobile: 0836 546556
Fax: 081-547 3022

FREDERIQUE LEFORT

21 Brewster Gardens
North Kensington
London W10 6AQ
Tel: 081-968 7250
Mobile: 0831 514401

COLIN BARKER

Contact: Francoise Tison

6A Pratt Street
Camden Town
London NW1 0AB
Tel: 071-380 1056
Fax: 071-380 0829
Mobile: 0831 528 100

STEUART GRAHAM

Contact: Kate Lampitt

The Studio
36 Grange Walk
London SE1 3DY
Tel: 071-237 7393
    0836 720435

JOHN TIMBERS v

Photographs people.

61 St. James's Drive
London SW17 7RW
Tel: 081-767 8386

Client: R.N.L.I.   Agency: Brookes & Vernons

Flat 2
4 Cromwell Road
Teddington
Middlesex TW11 9EH
England
Tel: 081-977 4064
Mobile: 0831 479302

**RUSSELL/PEROTTE
PHOTOGRAPHS**

Priory Studios
252 Belsize Road
London NW6 4BT
Tel: 071-625 4946

NADIA MACKENZIE v

Studio 111
Canalot Studios
222 Kensal Road
London W10 5BN
Tel: 081-964 0672
Fax: 081-960 7349
Mobile: (0831) 284473

Works on location, interiors, studio.
Clients include: Alan Crompton-Batt Associates,
Business Magazine, Conran Octopus, Elle Decoration,
Elle Magazine, GQ Magazine, Lynne Franks P.R.,
Maison Française, World of Interiors.

6 Hesper Mews
London SW5 0HH
Tel: 071-373 4896
Fax: 071-244 6091

Specialising in still life and flowers.

Studio 2
59 South Edwardes Square
London W8 6HW

Tel: 071-603 8331
Pager: 0459 11 4680
Fax: 071-603 9468

Art Director — Paul Morgan

GEOFF TOMPKINSON v

16 Gilbert Close
Rayleigh
Essex SS6 8QR
Tel: (0268) 770506
Fax: (0268) 770848
Mobile: (0836) 339924

Geoff specialises in location Science and Tech., producing striking images which combine high technical skills with creative originality. He has worked in 33 countries world wide. Clients include: Magazines — Sunday Times, Observer, GEO, Bunte, Ca M'Interesse, Avenue, Life, Genius, Smithsonian, Airone, Fakta, Science et Vie, Fortune. Corporate — Glaxo, Fisons, Wickes, Rank Zerox, Thorn. Design Groups — Valin Pollen, Tor Petersen. Sampson Tyrell, Timothy Guy Design, Drewrys, Fairfax. Stock available from: Derek Bayes, Aspect Picture Library. Tel: 071-736 1998.

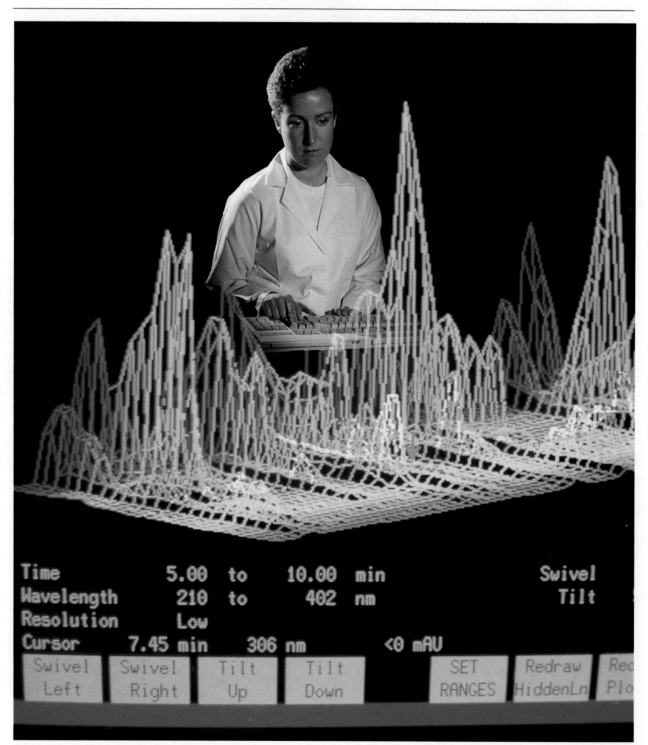

Caradon

Cray Electronics

Honeywell

Clients include:
National Westminster Bank
British Airways
Sony UK
Barings PLC
Cray Electronics
TNT-Worldwide
Attwoods
London International
Caradon
Honeywell
Lex
The Scottish Highland Railway Co.
Observer Magazine
Telegraph Magazine

Observer Magazine

Cecil Beaton

LEE HIGHAM

The Studio
46 Sherbrooke Road
London SW6 7QW
Tel: 071-381 2806
Fax: 071-385 9651
Mobile: (0831) 172 173

Specialist areas include all types of location work. Corporate literature involving people, industrial and still life. Corporate portraiture.

A wide range of black and white photography combining numerous print techniques.

The Scottish Highland Railway Co.

SCOTT MORRISON

Unit 3b
The Old Malthouse
Little Ann Street
Bristol BS2 9EW
Tel: Bristol (0272) 540360

FRANK FARRELLY

8 Cedar Way
Elm Village
Camley Street
London NW1
Tel: 071-387 5106
    081-341 5149
Represented by Julian Cotton
Tel: 071-486 3307
Fax: 071-486 6565

List of clients include: Lloyds Bank, Nurofen, Ford UK, Midland Bank, Trust House Forte, Dulux.

JEREMY YOUNG

10 Frithville Gardens
Shepherds Bush
London W12 7JN
Tel: 081-740 1317
Mobile: (0831) 117537

Location photography.
Landscape, Portrait, Architecture and Interiors for
Editorial, Corporate and Advertising.
Clients include: The Observer, C.M.G., Sunday Times,
Homes and Gardens, Telegraph Magazine,
Sunday Correspondent, Richard Ellis, Aukett Design,
Olympia & York, Wimpey, Price Waterhouse,
Departures Magazine, Alfa Lavall, Leiths Food,
Chesterfield Properties, Scidmore, Owings and Merrill.
Represented by Maggie Wise 071-629 1552.

ERIK PELHAM
A.M.P.A.

Represented by: Philip Millington-Hawes

79 Wilding Road
Wallingford
Oxon OXI0 8AH
England
Tel: (0491) 33568

Erik is a specialist location photographer, who concentrates on interiors using lighting. Studio work is also done, particularly on location, needing accurate colour. Working with an experienced assistant whose forte is good arrangement, he works for clients like: Hodder & Stoughton, Longmans & Eurobook — Publishers. Design — Architects Design Partnership, Heroes Design, Maxim Design for a large number of clients. The National Trust, interior designers, furniture companies and many others, eg Copthorne Hotels. He has done many commissions abroad eg books in Hong Kong for Longmans.

80 **CHRIS COLES**

Chris works from either his Drive-In Studio in Battersea
or on location for a wide range of clients including:
Mercedes Benz, Thorn EMI, British Telecom and
The Royal Bank of Scotland.

Havelock Studios
2 Havelock Terrace
London SW8 4AR
Tel: 071-627 0463
Fax: 071-738 8443

HARRY WILLIAMS

4 Brookside Close
Greenacres
Caerphilly
Mid Glamorgan
Wales, UK CF8 2RR
Tel/Fax: (0222) 861331
Car Phone (0836) 663432

PAUL DANCE

Space Building
Symes Mews
37 Camden High Street
London NW1 7JE
Tel: 071-388 2280
Mobile: 0860 376464

Advertising Photographer
Still Life, People and Multi images,
hates to be pigeon-holed.
Recent work includes:
British Aerospace, Abbey National,
Multi Broadcast, Myson Heating,
Accountancy Personnel, Sterling Guard,
Scotish Amicable, Letts and Premium Life....
Photographs shown are by kind permission of
Tony Stone Worldwide.

The
Food
Studio

A still-life photographic service, specialising in food, drink and related subjects. We have a fully equipped modern kitchen, and if necessary, can commission home economists, stylists and other services.

For more information please contact Nick Lee.

4th Floor
21-22 Great Sutton Street
London EC1V 0DN
Tel: 071-253 3085

PHIL MASTORES

47 Sandringham Road
London NW2 5EP
Tel: 081-451 5985

Area of Expertise:
Architecture, Interiors.
Clients include:
A & Q Partnership, BDP, Corporate Graphics Inc.,
EPR Partnership, Form Design, GRE Properties,
Hammond Design Partnership, Kaufman and Broad,
Knoll International, PSA, St. George Plc.,
Scott Brownrigg & Turner, Sheppard Robson & Partners,
Skidmore Owings & Merrill, Vitra Ltd.

The Rivers, Business Park. Scott Brownrigg & Turner.

Stockwell Bus Garage. HSAG.

PETER DAZELEY

The Studios
5 Heathmans Road
Parsons Green
London SW6 4TJ
Tel: 071-736 3171
Fax: 071-736 3356

My work covers still-life, cars, fashion, food, people and corporate literature both on location and in my large drive-in studio in Fulham.

Recent clients include: Abbey National, American Express, Benson and Hedges, Civil Aviation Authority, Citroen, Intercity, Mario Barutti, P & O, Pizza Hut, Pirelli Suits You, Telstar Records, Unilever, Volkswagen, Volvo, Yonex, Zales.

HOWARD BARTROP

56 Whitfield Street
London W1P 5RN
Tel: 071-637 4786

'Howard hates <u>still</u> life! So, by using innovative lighting techniques, projection, melting, motion, multi-image etc. he successfully enhances his compositions and adds another dimension. That success is bourne out by the following client list:
Alliance and Leicester, British Telecom, Church's Shoes, Debenham Tewson & Chinnocks, First Direct, Philips Hi-Fi The Royal Mail, Sammy's Film Services, Schroder, Sony, Tefal and many others.'

Pianos tuned while you wait.

OLI TENNENT

5B Cintra Park
Upper Norwood
London SE19 2LH
Tel: 081-653 9108
Fax: 081-653 9289
Mobile: 0836 564448

Specialist in sports and action photography with experience of working on advertising and editorial projects throughout Europe and the USA.
Some clients include: Steinlager, Sunseeker Powerboats, Unipart, Xerox, Arena, OMC, Shell Oils, Options, Uomo Mare Vogue, EMAP, British Airways, The Independent Magazine, The Observer.
Editorial training tailored to the needs of PR and advertising clients without inflated fees.

STEVE BISGROVE

Milan Based
c/o Elfande Art Publishing
Unit 39 Bookham Industrial Park
Church Street, Bookham
Surrey KT23 3EU
Tel: 0372 459559
Fax: 0372 459699

After several years experience as a London based photographer Steve is relocating to Milan, in what is an exciting and challenging opportunity to work in a city positioned very centrally for 1992, and the new markets in Eastern Europe. His specialisations include still-life, landscapes, architecture and interiors. In the studio, using creative lighting and strong backgrounds, he combines and emphasises the elements of texture, form and colour to produce striking images for ad. agencies, design groups and magazines. Another specialisation is his unusual infra-red technique, which has been used in advertisements, brochures and book-covers.

JO AGIS

Agent: Debut Art
28 Navarino Road
London E8 1AD
Tel: 071-254 2856
Fax: 071-241 6049

Recent clients include:
Domani Shoes (Grey Advertising),
The Royal Opera House, Coley Porter & Bell Design,
Vernon Oakley Design, Penguin, Secker & Warburg,
Methuen and EMI Music.

Commissioned by Grey Advertising for Domani Shoes.

94 **DEREK BERWIN**

45 Algers Road
Loughton
Essex IG10 4NG
England
Tel: (44) 081 502 0857
Fax: (44) 081 502 2874

Photographer/Traveller. Experience tells.
Alaska. Algeria. America. Antigua. Bahamas. Bahrain.
Barbados. Belgium. Brazil. Burma. Canada. Colombia.
Corfu. Cyprus. Denmark. Egypt. Fiji. Finland. France.
Germany. Gibraltar. Hawaii. Holland. Hong Kong.
Hungary. India. Iran. Israel. Italy. Jamaica. Japan.
Jordan. Kenya. Kuwait. Lebanon. Malta. Mauritius.
Mexico. Morocco. Nepal. New Zealand. Nigeria.
Norway. Oman. Pakistan. Portugal. Quatar. Russia.
Saudi. Senegal. St. Lucia. Sweden. Switzerland.
Thailand. Tobago. Trinidad. Tunisia. Turkey. U.A.E.
Venezuela. Virgin Isles. Yemen.

DEREK BERWIN

45 Algers Road
Loughton
Essex IG10 4NG
England
Tel: (44) 081 502 0857
Fax: (44) 081 502 2874

Photographer / Traveller. Experience tells.
Alaska. Algeria. America. Antigua. Bahamas. Bahrain.
Barbados. Belgium. Brazil. Burma. Canada. Colombia.
Corfu. Cyprus. Denmark. Egypt. Fiji. Finland. France.
Germany. Gibraltar. Hawaii. Holland. Hong Kong.
Hungary. India. Iran. Israel. Italy. Jamaica. Japan.
Jordan. Kenya. Kuwait. Lebanon. Malta. Mauritius.
Mexico. Morocco. Nepal. New Zealand. Nigeria.
Norway. Oman. Pakistan. Portugal. Quatar. Russia.
Saudi. Senegal. St. Lucia. Sweden. Switzerland.
Thailand. Tobago. Trinidad. Tunisia. Turkey. U.A.E.
Venezuela. Virgin Isles. Yemen.

JOHN HOLLINGSHEAD v

Represented by: BOS & Co

Tel: 071-287 8860
Studio: 117B Fulham Road
London SW3 6RL

Commercial Union

Jacob's Biscuits

BRIAN P. SPRANKLEN v

People and fashion.

Avalon
5 Pittbrook Street
Manchester M12 6LR
Tel: 061-274 3313
Fax: 061-273 2752

Avalon
5 Pittbrook Street
Manchester M12 6LR
Tel: 061 - 274 3313
Fax: 061 - 273 2752

![Photograph of a businessman at a cluttered desk surrounded by papers, telephones, an adding machine and office equipment.](image)

100 **DANIEL FAORO**

30 Upper Gulland Walk
Marquess Estate
London N1 2PF
Tel: 071-354 3994

People, performance, publishing, advertisng.
Clients include: Artsadmin, Tom Cat Design,
ES Magazine, Collins Publishers, Enigmatic Eve,
Hilton Grey, Von Magnet, Transworld, Maxell,
Theatre of Masque, Liz Ranken, Jacob Marley,
Stephen Taylor Woodrow, The Bombshells,
International Resque, Heart Break Angels,
Deb Thomas, Pandora Jockstrap.

DEREK GRACE

Shoots cars, still life, landscapes and people.
Subjects and format, both large and small.
Working principally for advertising agencies
and design groups.

77 More Close
St. Pauls Court
London W14 9BN
Tel: 081-748 0398

The Studio
4 Grafton Mews
London W1P 5LF
Tel: 071-388 1933
Fax: 071-387 5324

IAN HOOTON

Clients include: T.S.B., Alberto Vo5, L'Oreal, Virgin, Saatchi & Saatchi, Ilford Film, Wella, Schwarzkopf, Clairol, Optrex, Farah Clothing, American Vogue, Woman Magazine, Prima, Bella, Essentials, Womans Own, Woman and Home, Me, Just Seventeen.

103

Conran Studios
29-31 Brewery Road
London N7 9QN
Tel: 071-607 5386

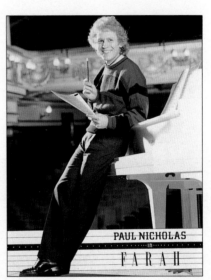

DEREK RICHARDS

Specialising in: people, travel, locations, corporate reports for Ad. Agencies and Design Groups.

1 Alma Studios
32 Stratford Road
London W8 6QF
England
Tel: 071-937 7533
Fax: 071-937 8285
Agent: Noelle Pickford
Tel: 071-584 0908

Smiths Industries/Tor Pettersen.

Grand Hotel Paris/Inter-Continental Hotel Corp.

Teachers Whisky/JWT.

RON BAMBRIDGE v

RONBAMBRIDGE
PHOT●GRAPHER

The three shots below form part of a specially commissioned calendar shot on 360 degree panoramic format. The work has since won the Kodak Award for best photography at the National Business Calendar Awards.

Clients include: British Rail, British Airports Authority, Peugeot, WH Smith, Tesco, Laing Construction, IPC Magazines, Anglian Water, Hill Holiday Boston, Michael Peters Group, Cogent, Evans Hunt Scott, Addison Design, RAC.

Holborn Studios
10 Back Hill
London EC1 5EN
Tel: 071-278 4311
Fax: 071-833 1377

360° panoramic

360° panoramic

360° panoramic

SANDRA LOUSADA

Susan Griggs Agency
2B, 101 Farm Lane
London SW6 1QJ
Tel: 071- 385 8112
Fax: 071-381 0935
Studio tel: 071- 727 7488
Studio fax: 071- 792 2306

Advertising, corporate and editorial, studio and location: children, fashion, health and beauty, portraits, crafts.
Clients include: Laura Ashley, Birthright, The Body Shop, Brides, BSB Dorlands, Century Hutchinson, Conran Mothercare, Country Living, Cow & Gate, Dorma, Fisher Price, Givenchy, Good Housekeeping, Great Ormond Street Hospital, Heinz, The Jenkins Group, Marie Claire, Next, Peper Harow, Playskool, Keith Shafto & Associates, Steel & Reeves, Tatler, Trickett & Webb.

Marie Claire/Revlon Ultima II.

The Body Shop Mamatota

JULIAN NIEMAN

Susan Griggs Agency
2B, 101 Farm Lane
London SW6 1QJ
Tel: 071-385 8112
Fax: 071-381 0935

Corporate and editorial, studio and location: travel, architecture, industry, hotels and restaurants, corporate portraits, children, still life, food.
Clients include: Astle Horman, British Tourist Authority, RSCG Conran Design, Country Life, European Travel & Life, Marriott Hotels, Mothercare, Next, Reader's Digest, Screentalk Productions, Smithsonian, Thames Water, TM Enterprises, Travel Holiday, The Wyatt Company.

Travel Holiday

Conran Design/Next

The Wyatt Company

ADAM WOOLFITT

Susan Griggs Agency
2B, 101 Farm Lane
London SW6 1QJ
Tel: 071-385 8112
Fax: 071-381 0935

Corporate and editorial people and places worldwide: travel, architecture, portraits, panoramics, aerials, reportage.
Clients include: British Tourist Authority, Cecil Denny Highton, European Travel & Life, The Guide Book Company, National Geographic, Pan Am Clipper, Reader's Digest, Sedgwick James, Smithsonian, Thistle Hotels, The Times, Travel Holiday, U.S. News & World Report, Weldon Owen Publishing.

The Guide Book Company: Turkey.

National Geographic.

MICHAEL
ST MAUR SHEIL

Corporate & Industrial Photography
Wyastone Cottage
Buckland
Oxfordshire SN7 8QR
Tel: (0367 87) 276
Fax: (0367 87) 641

Contact for advertising and editorial assignments:
Susan Griggs Agency
2B, 101 Farm Lane
London SW6 1QJ
Tel: 071-385 8112
Fax: 071-381 0935
Clients include: CEC Brussels, Charter Group, Costains, European Travel & Life, Inchcape, National Geographic, Merck Sharp & Dohme, Reader's Digest, RTZ, Shell Oil, South Western Bell Communications, Tor Pettersen, Unilever, Weldon Owen Publishing.

CEC Brussels.

Allied Steel & Wire.

Penwalt Inc.

MIKE RUSSELL

7 Canham Mews
Canham Road
London W3 7SR
Tel: 081-740 5357

Working mainly for the advertising business since the late seventies, Mike has shot most sorts of subjects for most sorts of agencies. His current folio includes work for award winning accounts such as Volvo, Saab, NatWest and Farleys.

MIKE LAYE

Shooting Star Pictures
23 Colville Terrace
London W11 2BU
Tel: 071-229 1756
(0860) 683880
24-hour word pager on
081-884 3344 ID: F951

I'm a photographer. I work happily and easily across all formats, in advertising, editorial or corporate and I make still-life & portraits of every description. My belief is that each brief is a problem waiting to be solved: The answer has to be a stunning image that fits the particular requirements of the job. If you want to categorise my style it is in that approach to the work. The Benson & Hedges photographs are an example — the organisers wanted a new way to photograph their Judges — and the finished 3-dimensional images are now on tour in the Gold Awards exhibition.

From a brochure for Palmbrokers

The Illustration Jury for the Benson & Hedges Gold Awards.

The Photography Jury

The Video Jury

DEREK LOMAS

69 Lambeth Walk
London SE11 6DX
England
Tel: 071-735 0993
Fax: 071-582 2379

Clients include:
Advertising Agencies
Design Groups
Conde Nast
G.Q.
Good Housekeeping
Marie Claire
Options
Womans Journal

STEVE WALLACE

Agent: Debut Art
28 Navarino Road
London E8 1AD
Tel: 071-254 2856
Fax: 071-241 6049

Recent clients include: Nationwide Anglia,
STC Communications, WEA Music, Phonogram,
Penguin Publishing, Secker & Warburg,
Heinemann, Accountancy Magazine,
Good Housekeeping Magazine.

117

Commissioned by Design In Action for STC Communications.

Commissioned by Secker & Warburg.

MIKE VAN DER VORD

Havelock Studios
2 Havelock Terrace
London SW8 4AR
Tel: 071-627 0463
Fax: 071-738 8443

Mike Van Der Vord shoots fashion, childrens fashion with a strong reportage influence both in the studio and on location. He has a great deal of experience in organising trips abroad. Recent foreign locations include France, Leningrad, Norway, Arizona Cyprus and several other Mediterranean countries.
In the studio Mike has developed a 'simulated daylight' technique which is very convincing. Samples of this plus all his other work can be viewed in his portfolio which is available on request.

120   **MICHAEL BANKS**

Represented in London by Julian Cotton.
Tel: 071- 486 3307
Fax: 071- 486 6565

Graphic, abstract, textural photography.

Corporate advertising, brochures, reports, murals.

Architectural, product, industrial, experimental.

Clients inlcude: Alfa Romeo, British Airways, Courtaulds, Grosvenor Estates, Grupo Banco Exterior, ICI, Nationwide Anglia, Norwich Union, RIBA, Rosehaugh Stanhope, Shimizu Development Co, Sony Music.

Abstract photo-library also available.

SIMON WARREN

Areas of expertise:
Architectural
Interiors
Industrial
Location

Tel: 071- 253 1711
Mobile: 0836 322711
Fax: 071- 248 3248

ED PRITCHARD v

144 Shaftesbury Avenue
Covent Garden
London WC2H 8HL
Fax: 071-839 7509
Tel: 071-836 0512

Studio and location photography for advertising and corporate clients, worldwide.

On these pages:
Singapore, Keppel shipyard
London, financial district at night
Hong Kong, The Regent at dawn
London, the Italian Embassy
Florida, tomato plantation.

JONATHAN KNOWLES
PHOTOGRAPHER v

Instinctive
Intuitive
Inexpensive
Inventive

37 Delaford Street
London SW6 7LT
Tel: 071-385 0188
Fax: 071-386 8785
Mobile: 0836 533933

"Diane, this must be where transparencies go when they die."

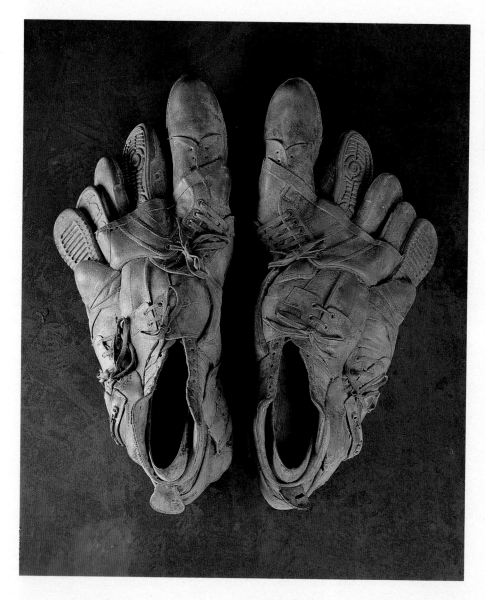

JAY MYRDAL v

JAM Studios
11 London Mews
Paddington
London W2 1HY
Tel: 071- 262 7441
Fax: 071- 262 7476

JAY MYRDAL v

KEITH FURNESS

Glamour
Beauty
Fashion

Calendars and Locational Photography a speciality.

Transparencies available from stock.

12 Tudor Avenue
Cheshunt
Herts. EN7 5AT
Tel: (0992) 38115
Fax: (0992) 25647
Mobile: (0831) 359515

PATRICK COLLANDRE

Studio "Oxygene" model making, room set, special effects together with photography are all created under the same roof in his Paris base Studio.

Contact: "Oxygene" Collandre Patrick

105 Avenue Parmentier
75011 Paris
Téléphone: (1) 48 06 06 13
Fax: (1) 43 57 89 38

BRENDAN MACNEILL

Kingsgate Workshops
110-116 Kingsgate Road
London NW6 2JG
Tel: 071-372 3372
Page: 081-884 3344 #A3372

JHON KEVERN v

Contact: Maggie Wise 071-629 1552

17 Novello Street
London SW6 4JB
Tel: 071-731 7438
Fax: 071-731 7438

ENRIC MONTÈ

C/ Premià 15, 1a
08014 Barcelona
Spain
Tel: 421 39 78
    422 66 33
Fax: 422 66 33

Specialist in advertising photography

DAVID SEED

Unit B
6 Sillavan Way
Salford
Manchester M3 6AE
England
Tel: 061-835 1902
Fax: 061-835 1028

Area of expertise:
Still life, advertising, special effects, food, drive-in and
overhead shooting facilities.

JAY LADVA

Studio 1
69 St. Marks Road
London W10 6JG
Tel: 081-968 9969
Fax: 081-964 0704

Represented by:
LONDON: Susan Ford
Pager: 0459 109828
Fax: 081-964 0704
MILAN: Laura Nocera
Tel: 498 0426
Fax: 481 93 788
PARIS: Allain Francois
Tel: 42 27 54 00
Fax: 46 22 00 24

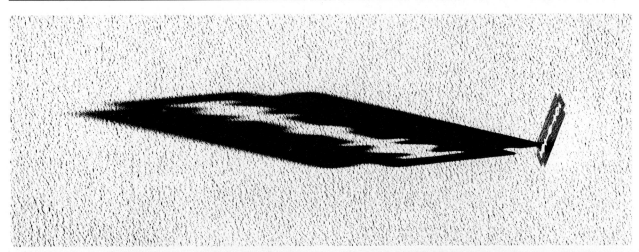

DEBI TRELOAR

43 Hartland Road
London NW6
U.K.
Tel: 071-328 0809

Agent: Susan Ford
Pager: 0459 109828

14 Premier House
Waterloo Terrace
London N1 1TG
Tel: 071-226 8727

Agent: Susan Ford
Pager: 0459 109828

Basement Studio
65 East Road
London N1 6AH
Tel: 071-490 2095
Fax: 071-490 4347

Norwich Union

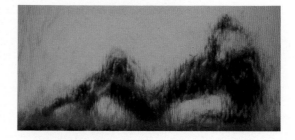

JASON SHENAI

Agent: Debut Art
28 Navarino Road
London E8 1AD
Tel: 071-254 2856
Fax: 071-241 6049

Recent clients include: Barclays, Allied Irish Bank, Access, TSB, IBM, Mercury Communications, Eurotunnel, Peat Marwick McLintock, The Body Shop, EMI Music, Decca International, Virgin Classics, The Observer, Penguin and Methuen.

Commissioned by
Summerhouse Communications for
Peat Marwick McLintock.

Commissioned by Forward Publishing for Datalogic.

Mark Davison

217 North End Road
London W14 9NP
Tel: 071-381 6707

COSMOS

COSMOS représente:
Tony Arciero — Jean-Louis Beaudequin — Eric De Cort —
Hans Hansen — Malcolm Leyland — Bruce Miller —
Manuel Prouteau — Paul Primeau — Mike Rausch —
Heimo Schmidt — Duncan Smith.
Contacts Paris: Valerie Denis
　　　　　　　　Cecile Rodrigue
　　　　　　　　Christian Marguerie
　　　　　　　　Thierry Cron
Contact Madrid: (1) 593-88-40.

7 Rue Sentou
92150 Surenes
France
Paris Tel: (1) 45-06-18-80
Madrid Tel: (1) 593-88-40

Contacts: Paris (1) 45-06-18-80 — Madrid (1) 593-88-40

Contacts: Paris (1) 45-06-18-80 — Madrid (1) 593-88-40

Contacts: Paris (1) 45-06-18-80 — Madrid (1) 593-88-40

Parano.

GOLF MEMPHIS
SÉRIE SPÉCIALE
à partir de **66.650** F*

Volkswagen. C'est pourtant facile de ne pas se tromper.

* Modèle présenté : Golf Memphis 55 ch/40 kW AM 90. Tarif au 08/09/89 - Peinture métallisée en option.

HEIMO SCHMIDT

Contacts: Paris (1) 45-06-18-80 — Madrid (1) 593-88-40

Contacts: Paris (1) 45-06-18-80 — Madrid (1) 593-88-40   Agent à Londres: Maggie Wise (71) 629-15-52

Contacts: Paris (1) 45-06-18-80 — Madrid (1) 593-88-40

Contacts: Paris (1) 45-06-18-80 — Madrid (1) 593-88-40

Contacts: Paris (1) 45-06-18-80 — Madrid (1) 593-88-40

COSMOS

7 Rue Sentou
92150 Surenes
France
Paris Tel: (1) 45-06-18-80
Madrid Tel: (1) 593-88-40

COSMOS représente:
Tony Arciero — Jean-Louis Beaudequin — Eric De Cort —
Hans Hansen — Malcolm Leyland — Bruce Miller —
Manuel Prouteau — Paul Primeau — Mike Rausch —
Heimo Schmidt — Duncan Smith.
Contacts Paris: (1) 45-06-18-80
　　　　　　Valerie Denis
　　　　　　Cecile Rodrigue
　　　　　　Christian Marguerie
　　　　　　Thierry Cron

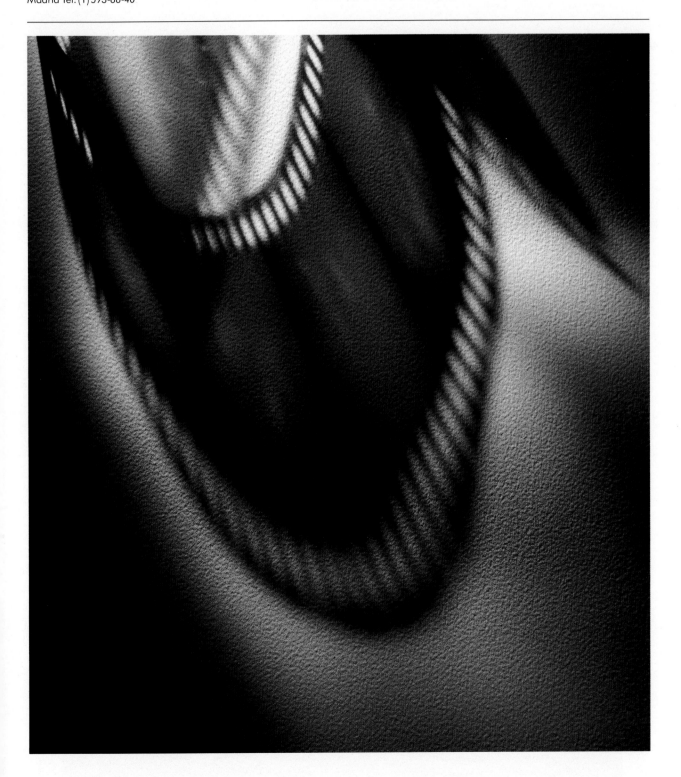

TIM HILL AFAEP V

59 Rosebery Road
Muswell Hill
London N10 2LE
Tel: 081 - 444 0609
Fax: 081 - 365 3588

Credits for pictures:
Bridal gifts courtesy of Ebury Press and Harrods.
Liquor shot courtesy of BSB Dorlands and Safeways.
Canned shot courtesy of Tim's portfolio.
Stylist — Zoë Hill. Assistant — Adrian Swift.
Home Economist — Simon Collins. E6 processing — Metro.
Paris Agents — Dixon — Nelson Tel: Paris 45 22 70 69.
Area of endeavour: Large format, still life and food
photography. My unreserved thanks go to my stylist Zoë
and my assistant Adrian. Also to my clients, old and new,
who indulge me in image making.

NEILL MENNEER AFAEP

Postscript Photographic Services
1 Argyle Street
Bath BA2 4BA
Tel: 0225 460063

Agent: Andrew Conningsby
Debut Art, Photographers and Illustrators Agents
28 Navarino Road, London E8 1AD
Tel: 071-254 2856 Fax: 071-241 6049

Neill specialises in corporate architectural and
location work.
My client list goes on and on. It includes: Coutts & Co.,
TSB and Midland Bank. However it is far less interesting
than my portfolio. If you would like to see (and could
use) creative location and architectural photography
then ring Andrew Conningsby.

Commissioned by Royle Murgatroyd for Anglian Water

Commissioned by RDDA for CNA reinsurance

MIKE BENNION

Agent: Debut Art
28 Navarino Road
London E8 1AD
Tel: 071-254 2856
Fax: 071-241 6049

No no no no no no no baby
I ain't askin' much of you
Just a big-a-big-a-big-a hunk o'love
Will do

Recent clients include: Sun Alliance, Trafalgar House,
Heath UK, ES Magazine, Penguin.

GEORGE SOLOMONIDES

77 Sugden Road
London SW11 5ED
Tel: 071-223 7885
    0860 645573

Architecture, Interiors, Models, Corporate, People, Landscape, Still Life, Fabrics, Furniture, Cars, Food and Toys.

Agent: Courtney Hildyard
Tel: 071-837 8783
    0860 301579

JOHN QUINN AFAEP

Tel: 0434 606822
Fax: 0434 608263
Mobile: 0860 671299

70% of work — location.
i.e. Holland, Belgium, Germany, Italy, Switzerland,
France (numerous), Spain (mainland & Balerics),
Canary Islands (numerous occasions — most of
the islands), U.S.A. (east & west coast areas), Tunisia,
Morrocco, Crete and of course England and Scotland.

Agent: Courtney Hildyard
Tel: 071-837 8783
     0860 301579

GRAHAM PRECEY

Studio 4
Kingsley House
Avonmore Place
London W14 8RY
Tel: 071-603 2690
Fax: 071-602 8616

Clients include: Aldi, Allied Breweries, American Express,
Arthur Bell Distillers, Asda, British Bakeries, Dairy Crest,
Ever Ready, Finncrisp, Gallahers, Gateways, Heinz,
International Masters Publishers, Lyons Maid,
Lyons Tetley, Nestlé, Prestige, Sainsburys,
Seagrams, Texaco, United Rum Merchants,
Wilkinson Sword, Wyeth.

Agent: Courtney Hildyard
Tel: 071-837 8783
      0860 301579

Backdrop by Nick Walton

BILLY

Babies · Animals · Children
London · Paris · New York

Studio 3
West Hampstead Studios
Sherriff Road
London NW6 2AR
Tel: 071-328 6000
Fax: 071-372 6060

Agent: Courtney Hildyard
Tel: 071-837 8783
0860 301579

Art Director: John White   *Agency: Paling-Ellis*

RAFAEL JOVER

DeVISU Fotografia
Ronda de San Pedro 74
Pral.2a
08010 Barcelona
España.
Tel: 93-302.19.30
Fax: 93-317.90.48

Studio 8
Abeerdeen Studios
22 Highbury Grove
London N5
Phone/Fax: 071-704 1408

33 Great Sutton Street
London EC1V 0DX
Tel: 071-253 7504
Fax: 071-251 9344
Agent: Ewan Dobbie
Tel: 071-251 9345

This Page:
Top: Client; Textdata Publishing.
Design Group; Identity.
Bottom: Client; Creative Handbook.
Design Group; Axis/The Yellow Pencil Company.

Opposite Page:
Top: Client; John Harris Design Consultants.
Bottom: Client; Athena Poster Campaign.

166 **CHRIS ARTHUR**

Corporate and Editorial
People and Places
Advertising
Entertainment
Industry

64 Gloucester Road
Kingston-upon-Thames
Surrey KT1 3RB
Tel: 081-546 4066

Simple Pleasures — Serious Stuff Crossing Watchers at Saumur

JAMES WEDGE

Church Gate Hall
Church Gate
London SW6 3LD
Tel: 071-731 1750
Fax: 071-731 7582

Clients include: Russell & Bromley, Clarks Shoes, Ravel, Wrangler Jeans, Gloria Vanderbilt Jeans, Pretty Polly Tights, Kayser, Berkshire Tights, Scholl Tights, Playtex, Emu Wool, Patricia Roberts Knitwear, Graff Jewellery, H. Samual, Wallis Shops, Next, Mothercare, Boots, Sainsburys, Marks & Spencers, Harrods, Harvey Nichols, C & A, Simpsons, Selfridges, Aquascutum, Austin Reed, Alexon, Pronuptia, Mary Quant, Slazenger, Rimmel, Lux, Pears Soaps, Ponds Creams, Avon, Yardley, Maybaline, Lichner, Pure & Simple, Coty, Fabergé, Polly Hair Products, Silverkrin, Cream Silk, Wella.

615a Green Lanes
London N13 4EP
Tel: 081-882 3427
Mobile: 0860 810147

JO FOORD v

Area of Expertise:
Children and people.

23/28 Penn Street
London N1 5DL
Tel: 071-256 0770/80
Mobile: 0860 309484
Fax: 071-729 3793

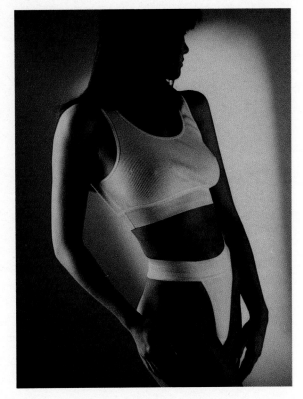

MARTIN CHAFFER

Battersea Park Studios
2 Shuttleworth Road
London SW11 3EA
Tel: 071-223 7119
Fax: 071-924 2958

MATTHEW J. BARLOW

Agent: Nicola Crawford
Tel: 071-729 3040
Fax: 071-613 2702

TONY MAY

92 Cranworth Gardens
London SW9 0NT
England
Tel: 071-587 0233
　　081-874 6677
Pager: 081-884 3344 pager code Tony 1

Represented by: Felicia Cohen
Tel: 071-490 0416

2nd Floor
11 Lever Street
London EC1V 3QU
Tel: 071-490 0952
Fax: 071-490 1895

176 **CRAIG HUNT**

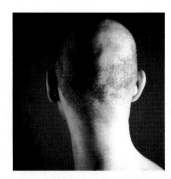

2-4 Vestry Street
London N1 7RE
England
Tel: 071-608 1005

Client: Next Directory 7
Agency: McCann-Erickson
Art Director: Steve Jones

MARIA ESPEUS

Guifré, 11
08001 Barcelona
Spain
Tel: (93) 242 20 06/07
Fax: (93) 329 16 47

Exhibitions:
1982 "Hola Barcelona" Institute of Estudios
Norteamericanos". Barcelona.
1990 "Fotografias" Sala Vinçon Barcelona.
Clients includes:
Spain: La Vanguardia Mujer, El Pais Dominical, El
Periodico, Fotogramas, Diagonal, Dunia, Elle, Marie-
Claire, Divina.
Italy:Uomo Vogue
Germany: Manipulator, select

PICTURES COLOUR LIBRARY LTD

10a Neals Yard
Covent Garden
London WC2H 9DP
Tel: 071-497 2034
Fax: 071-497 3070

Pictures is one of the fastest growing libraries in London with the freshest, most original material around. This is no accident. We work closely with our photographers and select only their best material. We listen to what you the client tell us when you give us a request.

Whether its people and their lifestyles, places, business, technology, scenics, food and pretty well everything else, we have it. So when you're next looking for a picture give us a call — we will give you our personal attention.

Write, phone or fax for a copy of our new brochure, or if you are in the area just drop in.

RAY ATKINS

Millrise Studios
Topcliffe
Thirsk
North Yorkshire YO7 3SQ
U.K.
Tel: (0845) 577874
Fax: (0845) 577744

Industrial
Fashion
Advertising
Corporate/Brochures
Telephone or Fax for mini portfolio.

PAUL REES

Agency: Alliance International
Client: Autistic Association
Descriptive portrait symbolising condition

Flashpoint Studios
8 Fitzroy Road
London NW1 8TX
Tel: 071-586 2935

RUPERT TRUMAN

Architecture, interiors and landscape.

15a Luttrell Avenue
Putney
London SW15 6PD
Tel: 081-788 6079
Mobile: 0831 361519

Clients: The Architects' Journal, Blakes Villas, Brittany Ferries, Carolyn Chester Interiors, Design Week, Dorland Business Communications, Mowlem Management, The National Trust, Redwood Publishing, Televisual.

PAUL HARVEY

Represented in Los Angeles by:
Liz McMillan
7316 West 90th Street
Los Angeles 90045
California, U.S.A.
Tel: (213) 641 0226
Clients include: Bank of Uganda, Charnos,
Du-Pont Howsons, Heineken, Lambs Navy Rum,
Perkins Engines, Range Rover, Seychelles Tourist Board,
Vickers Defence Systems

Tel: 0602 328328
Mobile: 0831 231440

Boadicea: For Vickers Defence Systems

ANDY WHALE v

Conran Studios
29-31 Brewery Road
London N7 9QN
Tel: 071-700 3252
    071-607 6423

DIDIER GUY

TCHAO STUDIO
Tel: 48 91 99 52
Tel: 48 44 29 53
Paris

ABBAYE DE LEFFE. L'INFINI D'UN PEU PLUS PRÈS.

ABBAYE DE LEFFE. L'INFINI D'UN PEU PLUS PRÈS.

PHILIP HABIB

2/4 Vestry Street
London N1 7RH
Tel: 071-490 4995
　　071-253 0824
Mobile: 0831 475555

Represented in London by: Charley Varley
Tel: 071-589 9968
Represented in Paris by: Dixon/Nelson
Tel: 45 22 70 69

DIXON NELSON v

25, Rue Lemercier
75017 Paris
Tel: (33.1) 45 22 70 69
Fax: (33.1) 45 22 70 59

Representing:
Hashi
Philip Habib
Mark Hall
Tim Hill
Peter Lavery
Butch Martin
Philip Pace
Keith Shillitoe
Jimmy Wormser

HASHI

Dixon Nelson — The Photographers Agent
25, Rue Lemercier 75017 Paris

Tel: (33.1) 45 22 70 69
Fax: (33.1) 45 22 70 59

KEITH SHILLITOE

Dixon Nelson — The Photographers Agent
25, Rue Lemercier 75017 Paris

Tel: (33.1) 45 22 70 69
Fax: (33.1) 45 22 70 59

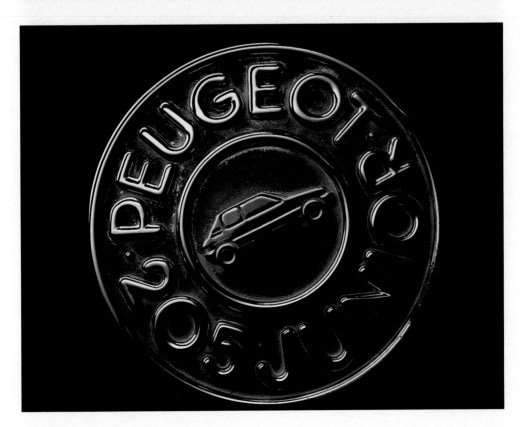

Dixon Nelson — The Photographers Agent
25, Rue Lemercier 75017 Paris

Tel: (33.1) 45 22 70 69
Fax: (33.1) 45 22 70 59

Dixon Nelson — The Photographers Agent
25, Rue Lemercier 75017 Paris

Tel: (33.1) 45 22 70 69
Fax: (33.1) 45 22 70 59

Dixon Nelson — The Photographers Agent
25, Rue Lemercier 75017 Paris

Tel: (33.1) 45 22 70 69
Fax: (33.1) 45 22 70 59

N.B. ESTUDIO FOTOGRAFICO

ESTUDIO FOTOGRAFICO

Photography: Alberto Nicolas
Production: Eduardo Báras

Advertising photography: still life, people, super productions and locations.

Contact: A. Nicolás/E. Báras

Ferrán Puig, 50
08023 Barcelona
Tel: (93) 21 36 464
Fax: (93) 21 33 253

Photographers Agent
14-15 D'Arblay Street
London W1V 3FP
Tel: 071-287 9614
Fax: 071-494 3670

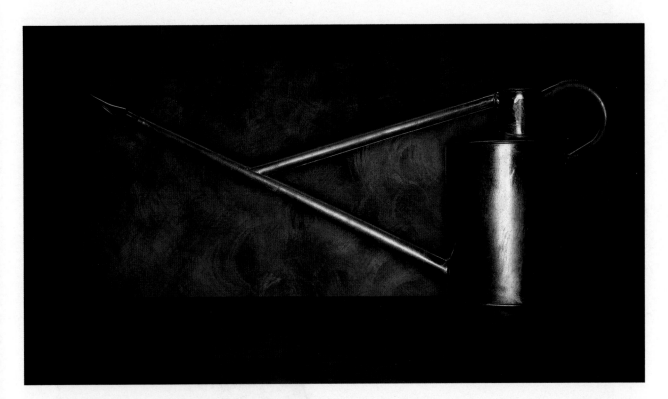

OWEN SMITH

EITAN LEE AL

MICHAEL CROCKETT

BEN RICE

BEN RICE

196   **MICHAEL MICHAELS**

13 Deane House
27 Greenwood place
London NW5 1LB
Tel: 071- 267 2846
Fax: 071-485 5335

"Specializes in Food and Still Life photography for editorial, packaging and advertising clients who include Asda, American Express, Bass, British Telecom, Bowater Foil, Colmans, Country Homes and Interiors, Dairy Cream Council, Hertz Rent a Car, Japan Airlines, KLM Airlines, Lyons, Mc Cormicks, Marks & Spencers, Me, Nulon Hand Cream, Royal Bank of Scotland, Swatch, Safeway, Silver Spring, Sodastream, Suzi Wan, Uncle Bens, Whitworths, Womans Journal and Womans World."

GRAHAM TANN

17/21 Emerald Street
London WC1N 3QL
Tel: 071-405 7900
Fax: 071-404 2072

Corporate Work,
Cars,
Advertising,
Editorial,...
Photography!!!

197

IAN FRASER

Fraser Studios
Unit 15 / 4
Botley Works
Botley
Oxford OX2 OLX
Tel: 0865 250088
Fax: 0865 791402

SPECIALITY. — CARS AND OTHER VEHICLES.
Painted backgrounds and sets.

200 **GRAHAM SEAGER**

Interiors
Still life
Roomsets

45-47 Clerkenwell Road
London
EC1M 5RS
Tel: 071-608 2729

RSCG Conran Design

FRÉDÉRIC HUIJBREGTS

Agent: Laurence Devaux
28, 30 Rue des Peupliers
75013 Paris
France
Tel: (33) 1. 45. 89. 11. 11
Fax: (33) 1. 45. 80. 81. 19

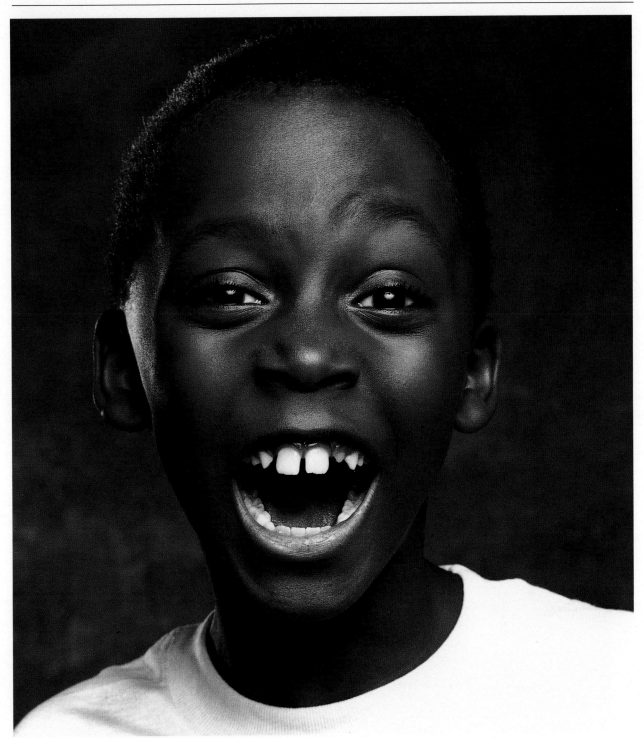

KODAK T.MAX P 3200. Advertising Campaign.

ISABELLE ROZENBAUM
ET FREDERIC CIROU

AGENT: Laurence Devaux
28, 30 rue des Peupliers
75013 Paris
France
Tel: (33) 1. 45. 89. 11. 11
Fax: (33) 1. 45. 80. 81. 19

96 Park Avenue South
London N8 8LS
Tel: 081-341 2921

PHIL TROST

53-55 Bayham Place
London NW1 0ET
England
Tel: 071-383 2073
Fax: 071-383 2109

Art Direction: Joseph McGlennon

MARTIN FORREST

Tel: 071 - 261 0360
Pager Number: 0459 858066

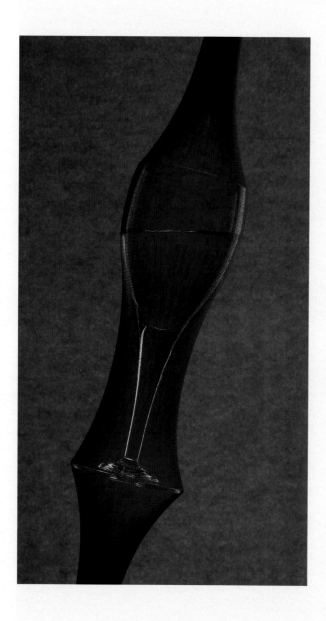

BENEDICT CAMPBELL

Fraser Studios
Unit 15 / 4, Botley Works
Botley
Oxford OX2 0LX
Tel: (0865) 250088
Fax: (0865) 791402

Photographic Trompe L'oeile
Painted backgrounds
Cars, Bikes
Fashion
Still Life

Fiat 328 GTB Tipo

COLIN MILLS

23-28 Penn Street
London N1 5DL
England
Tel: 071-739 7694
Fax: 071-739 6543

Area of expertise:
Still Life, Roomsets, Special Effects.
Clients include:
British Telecom,
Heuga International,
House of Fraser,
Rank Xerox,
Bentalls,
IBM,
Phillips,
Marlow Wade.

GEOFF SMITH v

The Old School
No. 1 Thirsk Street
Ardwick Green
Manchester M12 6HP
Tel: 061-273 7489
Fax: 061-274 3449

Specialising in fashion and people, in studio/sets or location. Good daylight studio and excellent organisational backup.

IAN BRADSHAW

Speciality:
People who hate being photographed!
Clients include:
BBC, MEB, Millicom Int.,
Jefferson Smurfit Group,
London Edinburgh Trust PLC.,
Highland Park.

Represented by
Sandie
Tel: 081-861 4383
Mobile: 0836 311339

MATTHEW WEINREB v

The Studio
16 Millfield Lane
London N6 6JD
England
Tel: (44) (0) 81 -340 6690
Fax: (44) (0) 81 -341 0441
Mobile: (44) (0) 836 679694
France: (33) 62652143

I specialise in photographing architecture, interiors, landscapes and cityscapes, though my work has encompassed a fair bit of portraiture as well. My clients include advertising agencies, design groups, architects, interior designers, PR companies and magazines.

IAN SOUTHERIN

PHOTOGRAPHER **IAN SOUTHERIN**

Specialist in powerful images for corporate brochures and annual reports.

50b Egerton Park
Rock Ferry
Birkenhead L42 4QZ
Tel: 051 644 6896
Europe 44 51 644 6896

OLIVER BENN

Hackhurst Farm
Lower Dicker
Hailsham
East Sussex BN27 4BP
Tel: (0323) 844267
Fax: (0323) 442700

Interiors, Architecture, Landscapes, People in situ, General location photography.

Clients include Weidenfeld and Nicholson, Cassells, Wiltshier Group, Inchbald School of Design, Direct Image Design, Marketeer PLC, Oracle Advertising, Sir Frederick Gibberd, Coombes and Partners; and various magazines.

I am often in the London area.
I do my own E6 processing for maximum quality.

ANNA LOSCHER

Juan Ramón Jiménez, 22
28036 Madrid
Spain
Tel: 010 341 259 9015

Member of the Madrid Association of Advertising and Fashion Photographers. German, studio in Madrid since 1979.
Specialization in B/W, Still life and portrait.
Works mainly for magazines and editing houses in Spain, Germany and Switzerland.
Also advertising photography.

BAY HIPPISLEY v

16 Lion Yard
Tremadoc Road
London SW4 7NF
Tel: 071-978 2552

ZAFER BARAN

Abstract and experimental photography: still life and people.

Clients include: British Airways, Royal Bank of Scotland, Eagle Star Insurance, BP, Metropolitan Home, Decca Records, BBC, Woolworths, Atlantic Estates, Wolff Olins, Midland Bank, Penguin Books, Lillywhites, BICC Technologies, Electra Investment Trust, The World Markets Company, Calor Gas.

1 Venn Street
London SW4 0AZ
Tel: 071-627 4225/622 9700

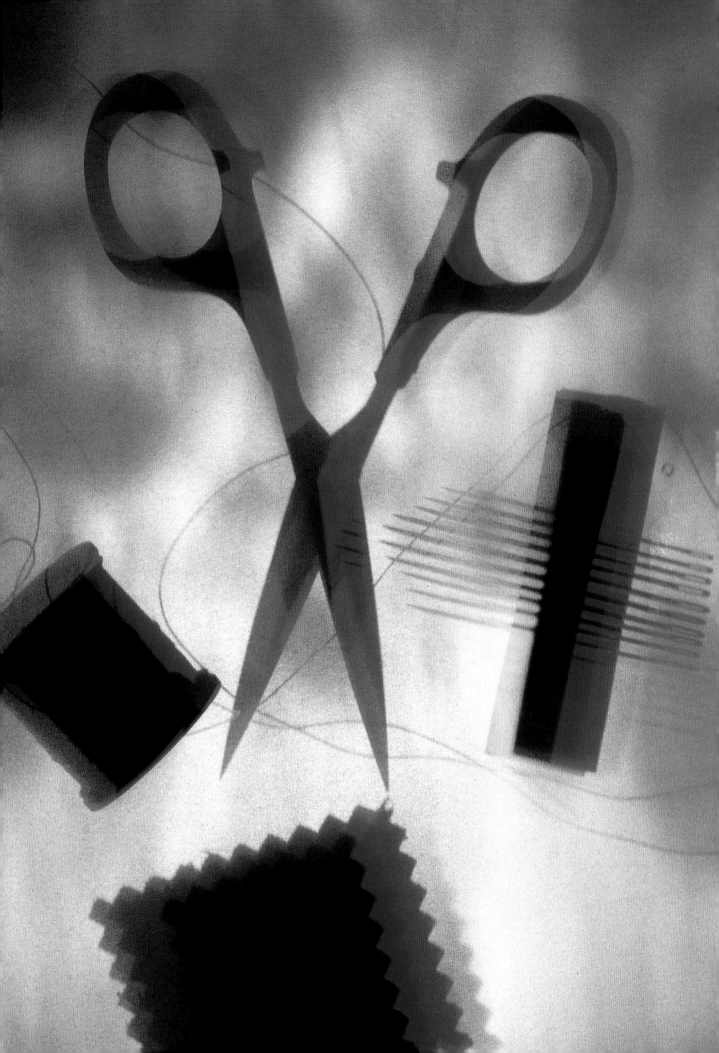

ANDREW PUTLER, JO PUTLER

182 Highbury Hill
London N5 1AU
Tel: 071-226 9911
Mobile: 0836 283284

- Annual reports, PR, portraits, architecture (incl. models), studio still lives.
- Well equiped studio with large, medium and 35mm formats.
- Bilingual in French.

"With thanks to Securicor"

CHRIS HOPPER

Specializing in people, fashion, corporate reports and financial services, for brochures and advertising.

60 St. Stephens Gardens
London W2 5NJ
Tel: 071-221 1621
Fax: 071-221 1621
Mobile: 0831 449582

Courtesy of 'Telsis Communications'

KEN KIRKWOOD
AFAEP

The Barns
Harborough Road
Stoke Albany
near Market Harborough
Leicestershire LE16 8PY
Tel: 085 885 424
Fax: 085 885 455

K **k**

I specialise only in <u>not</u> specialising. I'll photograph almost anything, almost anywhere — from tough, dirty industry to delicate, fashionable interiors. My client list reads like a Who's-Who of big names in business, property companies and designers. I'd like to add your name to that growing list of satisfied clients.

DAVID GILL

7 Aberdeen Studios
22 Highbury Grove
London N5
Tel: 071 -354 1561
Fax: 071 -354 1552

222 **NICK DOLDING**

28/29 Great Sutton Street
London EC1V 0DS
Tel: 071 · 490 · 2454
Fax: 071 · 251 · 3843

AGENTS:
LONDON
Sue Young and Camilla
Tel: 071 · 262 · 0189
Fax: 071 · 262 · 2160

HAMBURG
Marion Enste-Jaspers
Tel: 040 · 222 · 226
Fax: 040 · 221 · 062

Amex. O and M Direct

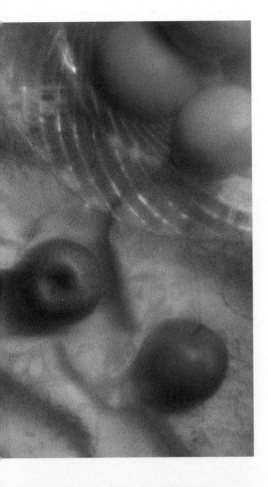

B.M.P. Davidson Pearce

TIM IMRIE

Contact: Producer/Anna Tait
Studio & Office:
24 Brook Mews North
Lancaster Gate
London W2 3BW
Tel: 071-402 7517
Fax: 071-723 0454

Tim Imrie's studio is conveniently situated near the West End, a stone's throw from Lancaster Gate Tube Station on Hyde Park. A stone's throw in the other direction reaches Paddington Tube and Rail Station. With set building facilities and props storage, his large, high ceilinged studio has an excellent kitchen attached, enabling him to meet the requirements of a wide range of clients in the fields of Interiors, Still Life and Food photography. He also undertakes location Food and Interiors photography in the UK and abroad.

Client: Frances Lincoln Publishing 'Paper Magic'

Client: Selfridges

Opposite — Client: House and Garden

TIM WREN

23 Bromells Road
London SW4
Tel: 071-720 5099

represented by
Julian Cotton
12 Thornton Place
London W1H 1FL
Tel: 071-486 3307
Fax: 071-486 6565

Specialises in Car and Truck photography.

Recent clients include:
Jaguar
Land Rover
Volvo
Ford
The Sunday Times
Car Magazine

ANDY SEYMOUR v

Specialist in: Still life
Food
Children
Call for folio.

82 Princedale Road
Holland Park
London W11 4NL
Tel: 071 - 221 2021
Fax: 071 - 792 0702

227

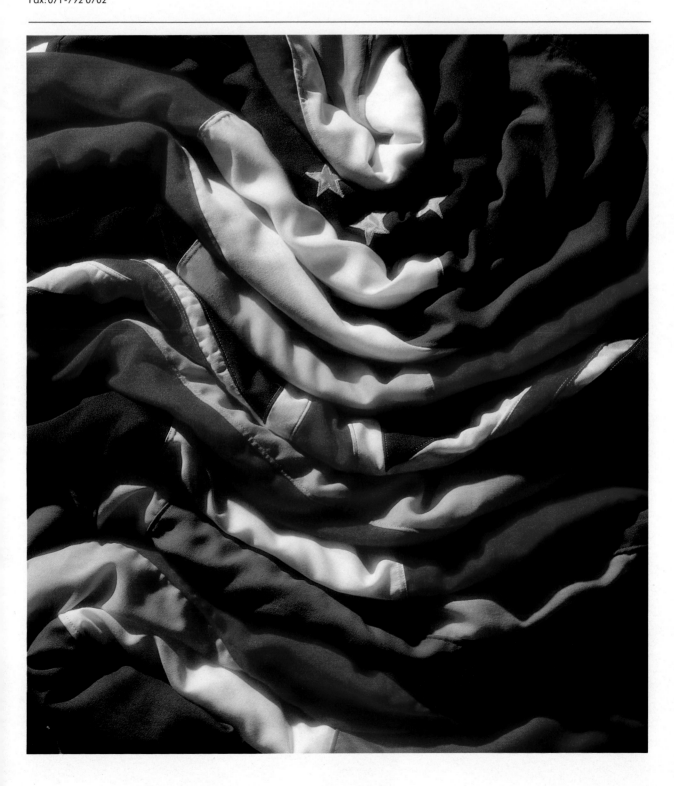

DAVID ASH v

Shaftesbury House
13 / 14 Hoxton Market
Coronet Street
London N1 6HG
Tel: 071 - 739 0990
Fax: 071 - 739 2321
Represented in Paris by DDA
Tel: (1) 45 20 74 16
Fax: (1) 45 20 72 13

Clients include:
AB Littleman, Britvic, Peter Black, Cuprinol, Enterprise
Oil, KP, Marks & Spencer, Mirror Publishing, Manu Life,
Nat West, Pepsi, Sharwoods, 7 up, Vispring, Mr Wobbler.

ASHLEY GIBBONS

Tel: (0272) 724304
Fax: (0272) 719889
Car: (0836) 651740

If a picture paints a thousand words, then strong creative photography should allow us to do without words altogether. It would therefore be pointless to talk about our commitment to meeting our clients' precise requirements, or to point out that we, like yourself, understand the importance of working to deadlines. The fact that we have been established in Bristol since 1987 (having previously been in London) would be of little interest, as would the fact that our large well equipped studio can accomodate almost any brief you care to give us. Instead, we'd rather let the pictures tell the story...

SIMON BATTENSBY

Studio 28
"Waterside"
44-48 Wharf Road
London N1 7SH
Tel: 071-251 4223

Chairman of Wembley Stadium PLC

Summit PLC

British Rail

**AMANDA
RAMSBOTTOM
PHOTOGRAPHERS'
AGENT**

Tel: 071 -323 2291
Fax: 071 -323 3292

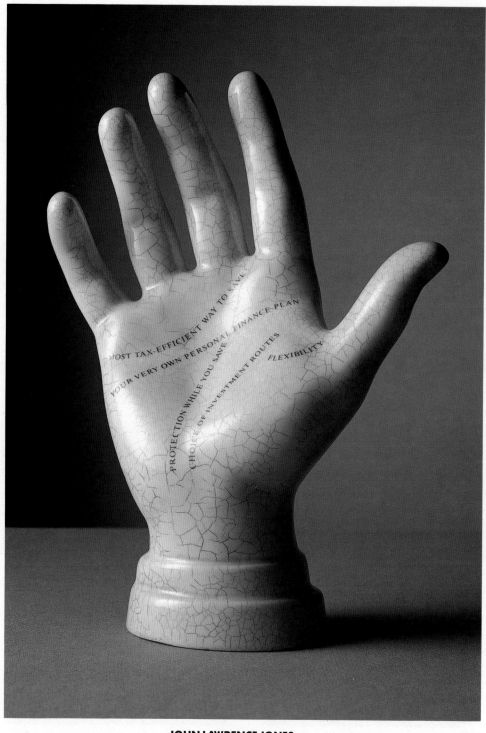

JOHN LAWRENCE JONES

CHARLIE STEBBINGS

2-4 Vestry Street
London N1 7RH
Tel: 071-253 0003
Fax: 071-490 1317

HOWARD
KINGSNORTH

7 Plough Yard
London EC2A 3LP
Tel: 071-247 4765
Fax: 071-247 4836
Mobile: 0860 418378

Specialist problem solving photography: in the studio
and on location.
Also directing through Cassar Films:
At 39/43 Brewer Street, London W1
Tel: 071-434 2841 Fax: 071-439 3793

"N.O.W. THAT'S WHAT I CALL GRIPPING."

PETER BEAVIS

Tel: 071-624 4884
Mobile: 0860 758861

Clients include:
B.P.
C.B.M.E.
Dewe Rogerson
Fred Perry
Mercury
M.G.M.
Olivetti
Sky T.V.
Wessex Water

Represented by
Debut Art
28 Navarino Road
London E8 1AD
Tel: 071 - 254 2856
Fax: 071 - 241 6049

commissioned by
CODA Records

commissioned by
MICRO - DECISION
magazine

SEAN PRESTON

Tel: 071 -635 0446

**BARBARA
BELLINGHAM**

Agent: Debut Art
28 Navarion Road
London E8 1AD
Tel: 071-254 2856
Fax: 071-241 6049

Recent clients include:
Barclays Bank, Morgan-Grenfell Laurie, Spicer-Oppenheim, 3M, Hilton Hotels, Sunday Times Mag., The Observer Mag., Sunday Telegraph Mag., The Radio Times, The Listener, Vogue Homme, Elle Mag., Penguin Publ., Creative Review.

Commissioned by Eurobusiness magazine for cover feature on the sponsorship business

GAVIN COTTRELL

16 Elizabeth Mews
London NW3 4UH
Tel: 071-586 8625
Fax: 071-586 8978
Agent: Julian Cotton
Tel: 071-486 3307
Fax: 071-486 6565

Area of expertise:
Drinks
Still Life
Clients include:
Distillers
Bulmers
Bass
Whitbread
Courvoisier

CARL WARNER

25 Malvern Mews
London NW6 5PT
Tel: 071-328 6534
Fax: 071-625 0221

Carl Warner age 28, pictured here working on a recent beer shot. "Sometimes it is better to employ the simplest of techniques to achieve ones end!". It is this kind of self sacrifice, meticulous attention to detail and thorough personal commitment to a shot that makes him one of the most difficult people to talk to on the phone. So why don't you call his agent?

Agent: Damien Birtwistle
25 Grosvenor Crescent Mews
London SW1X 7EX
Tel: 071-235 4789 Fax: 071-823 1032

NICK CARMAN v

32 Great Sutton Street
London EC1V 0DX
England
Tel: 071-253 2863
Fax: 071-250 3375

Areas of expertise:
Food Specialist
Clients include:
Asda, Sainsbury, Tesco, Marks & Spencer, Nestlé,
Landor Associates, Publicis, Mappin & Webb,
National Magazines, IPC, Octopus Books, Heinz and
Del Monte.

KEES TABAK

Contact: Truus Huibers

Egelantiersgracht 95
1015 RE Amsterdam
The Netherlands
Tel: 09 31 (0)20 6229476
Fax: 09 31 (0)20 6259065

MALCOLM LEYLAND v

10a Lant Street
London SE1 1QA
Tel: 071-378 7544
Fax: 071-378 1867

London Agent:
Maggie Wise
Tel: 071-629 1552
Mobile: 0836 371851
Paris Agent:
Valerie Dennis
Cosmos. Tel: (331) 45061880
Below: For Madame Figaro magazine.
Top Right: For British Steel poster.
Middle Right: For Tupperware brochure cover.
Bottom Right: For Virgin Retail packaging.

ADRIAN TURNER

Unit 2
29-42 Windsor Street
Brighton
East Sussex BN1 1RJ
Tel: (0273) 821840
Fax: (0273) 735822

TIM MOTION v

91 St. Mark's Road
London W10 6JS
Tel: 081-960 6102
Mobile: 0836 55 11 36

Experienced in architectural, location and aerial photography, as well as interiors and portraiture, for Advertising, Annual Reports and Brochures.
Extensive Stock Library of Jazz and Blues Artistes, and Travel material. Speaks Portuguese, Spanish and French.
Clients include: Kuwait Airways, Berisford International, Woolworths, National Data Corporation, Stanhope Rosehaugh, PPP, Barbados Board of Tourism, Indonesian Tourist Board, Goldman Sachs, Pelican PR, magazines and newspapers.

PETER DAZELEY

The Studios
5 Heathmans Road
Parsons Green
London SW6 4TJ
Tel: 071-736 3171
Fax: 071-736 3356

My work covers still-life, cars, fashion, food, people and corporate literature both on location and in my large drive-in studio in Fulham.

Recent clients include: Abbey National, American Express, Benson and Hedges, Civil Aviation Authority, Citroen, Intercity, Mario Barutti, P & O, Pizza Hut, Pirelli Suits You, Telstar Records, Unilever, Volkswagen, Volvo, Yonex, Zales.

CAMERA 2

Contact: Chris Rose
           Derek Welbourne
Studio House
David Street Yard
Off Water Lane
Leeds LS11 5QA
Tel: (0532) 428060
Fax: (0532) 428455

Still life, food, fashion, cars, roomsets, special effects
four Photographers, 5000ft^2 studio, 2 mins from M1.
Drive in fully coved.
Full backup services, stylists, setbuilders, modelmakers,
processing.

PAUL WEBSTER

2C Macfarlane Road
Shepherds Bush
London W12 7JY
England
Tel: 081-749 0264
Fax: 081-740 8873

Clients include: Asda, Marks & Spencer, Tesco, Sainsburys, United Biscuits, Jacobs, Batchelors, Nestlé, Heinz.
And also many still-life clients including:
Mappin & Webb, Gucci, Carvela, Du Pont, Lloyds Bank, National Westminster Bank, Richard Ogden, C&A and many more.
Paris Agent — DDA, Blanca Maisonelle, Paris 45207416.

Blue plate & crumbs — Shot for McVities

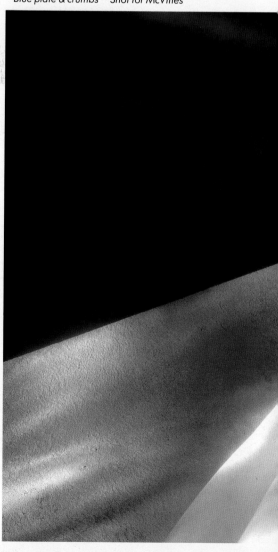

Candles & Cake — Shot for portfolio

Egg on plate — Shot for the Benson and Hedges Exhibition

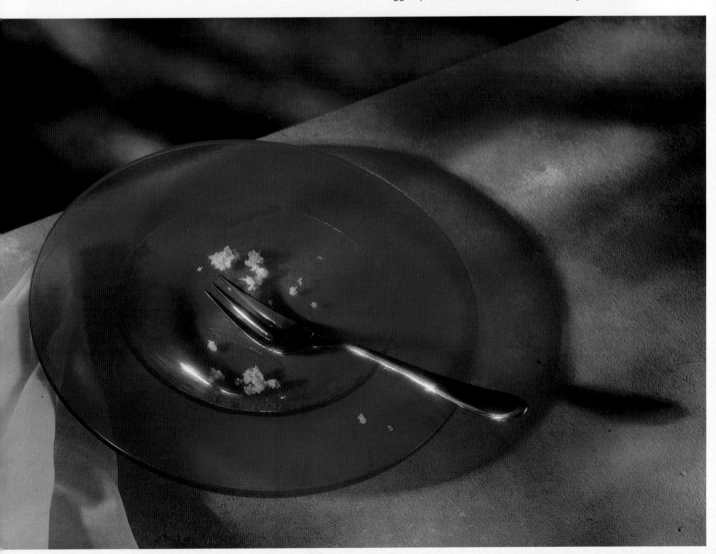

THE PETER BAILEY COMPANY v

► THE PETER BAILEY COMPANY REPRESENTS

MARTIN LANGFIELD

TELEPHONE 071 935 2626   FACSIMILE 071 935 7557

GULLACHSEN

GRANT SYMON

TELEPHONE 071 935 2626   FACSIMILE 071 935 7557

MICHAEL HARDING

TELEPHONE 071 935 2626   FACSIMILE 071 935 7557

► **THE PETER BAILEY COMPANY REPRESENTS**

TELEPHONE 071 935 2626   FACSIMILE 071 935 7557

JAN BALDWIN

Tel: 081 - 674 4081

JOHN DAVID BEGG

Tel: 071-354 2446
Mobile: 0836 353 339

Marples Developments

Cassidy Road
London SW6 5QH
Tel: 071-736 6205
     071-736 7694

See illustration page 419.

NEAL WILSON

33 Great Sutton Street
London EC1V 0DX
Tel: 071-253 7491
Fax: 071-490 2558
Agent: Ewan Dobbie
Tel: 071-251 9345

Design Groups: Tor Pettersen & Partners,
Sampson Tyrrell, Addison, Fine White Line, Thumb,
Landor, Benjamin Roundtree Reports, Jenkins Group,
Small Back Room.
Clients: Abbey National, Beechams, Crown Television,
Enterprise Oil, Fishermans Friend, Granada,
Midland Bank, Mercury, Post Office Counters,
Nat. West Bank, Storehouse, Smith & Nephew, Evode,
Bupa, Plessey, Bonhams, The Salvation Army, The Wing
Fellowship Trust, The Health Education Authority &
The Department of Health.

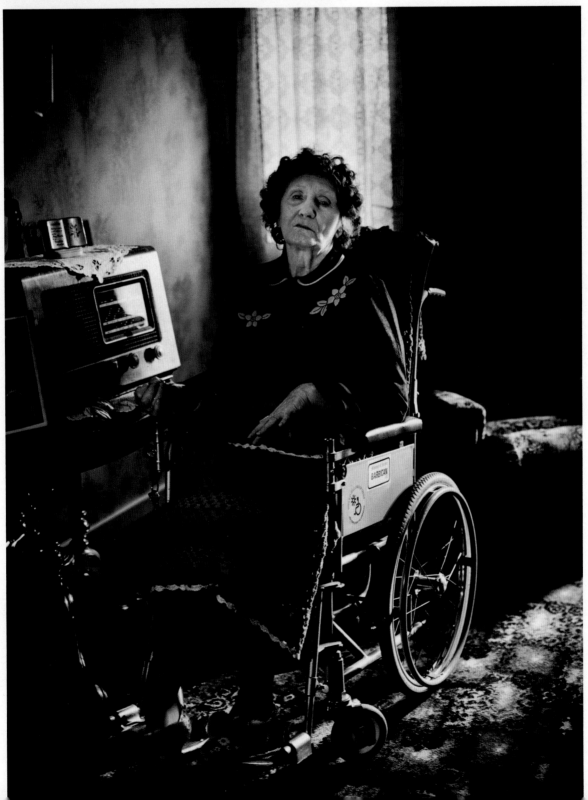

266 **GARETH TREVOR v**

Agent:
Denise Chapman
Tel: 071 - 495 3048
Fax: 071 - 493 4317

6 - 8 Sedley Place
London W1R 1HG
Tel: 071 - 493 8735

DAVID PREUTZ

6-8 Gwynne Road
London SW11 3UW
Tel: 071-350 1733
Fax: 071-924 2456
Mobile: 0831 350725

Some recent clients include:
American Express
Barclays Bank
Burberrys, Gonzalez Byass
Helena Rubenstein, ICI
International Distillers
Newcastle Brown
Thorn EMI Lighting
Toyota, Yashica / Contax
New 2500 square foot studio with drive in facility &
unrestricted parking.

PHOTOGRAPHERS
agent

3B Healey Street
London NW1
Tel: 071-482 4346
Agent: BOS & Co.
Tel: 071-287 8860

Credits
Left hand page top: Sun Alliance
Bottom: Electricity Privatisation
Right hand page top L & R: BUPA
Bottom: BOC

DAVID STEWART

Agent:
Noelle Pickford
Tel: 071-584 0908

26-27 Great Sutton Street
London EC1V 0DF
England
Tel: 071-608 2437

26-27 Great Sutton Street
London EC1
England
Tel: 071-251 5333
Mobile: 0836 753980
Fax: 071-253 0319

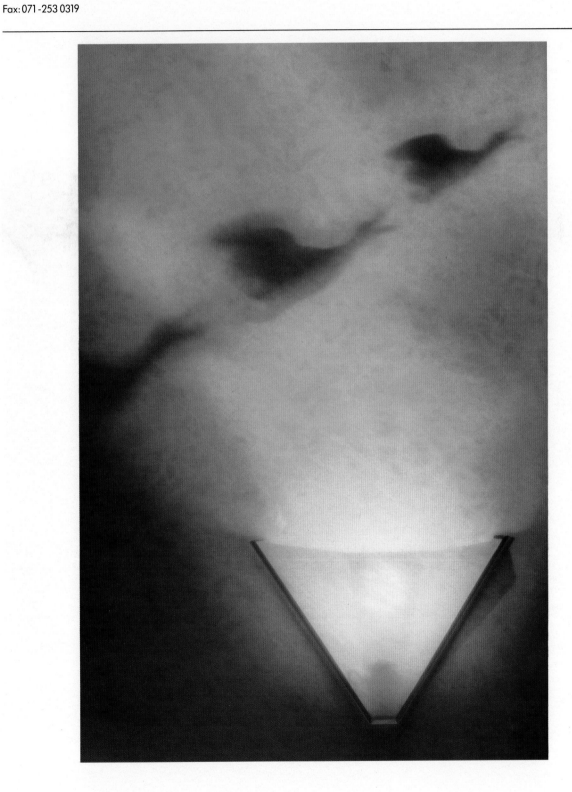

TONY BOWN

35 Adam & Eve Mews
London W8 6UG
Tel: 071-938 1967
Fax: 071-937 7254

My ideal brief:
Still-Life requiring technical*
execution and the creation of
mood and atmosphere....
....please!
*Double exposure, movement,
effects etc.

LARRY BRAY

7 Kensington High Street
London W8 5NP
England
Tel: 071-938 3402
Mobile: 0860 800180
Fax: 071-937 2379

Location photography for Advertising, Corporate, Design and Editorial.

Clients include:
American Express, Barratt, Boots, Brent Walker Group, British Gas, British Telecom, Butlins, Canadian Imperial Bank, Europa Hotels, Harrods, Innoxa, Kodak, MGM Assurance, Otis, Pilsbury UK, Ramada International, Reed International, Sarova Hotels, Schlumberger, Southern Electric, TSB, Unilever, Woolworth.

ROB BROWN

18-22 Barnsbury Street
London N1 1PN
Tel: 071-354 3713
Pager: 081-884 3344 Code F3333
Fax: 071-704 1234

Rob specialises in Architectural Photography,
Interiors, People 'in situ', Industrial and occasionally,
Aerial Photography. He covers annual reports,
corporate brochures, letting brochures and advertising
generally and works both home and abroad.
Recent clients include: BAA plc, Seifert Group, Beard
Dove Ltd, Hodge Associates, Independent Design, Bovis
Construction, Fitzroy Robinson, Broad St. Advertising,
Holmes and Marchant and Bell Design.
To see his portfolio or discuss your photographic needs
ring for a chat.

GEORGE TAYLOR
PHOTOGRAPHY

GEORGE TAYLOR | PHOTOGRAPHY

It is not a question of the traditional view but more a question of craft, interperative, positive and pro-active.

Studio 19
10-11 Archer Street
London W1V 7HG
Tel: 071-734 4461
Fax: 071-734 8771

JIM FORREST

82 Chestnut Grove
London SW12 8JJ
Tel: 081 -673 0936
Fax: 081 -675 0091
Mobile: 0836 738841

Direct Input / B.P.C.C

Malcolm Rifkind/Director Magazine

Lombard Odier/Swiss Bank

Royal Mail / Sampson Tyrrell

SOLANGE GAULIER

Tél.: 33. 1. 47. 90. 02. 42
Télex: 33. 1. 47. 28. 71. 91

Agent: FLUO
Marie-Christine Burlot
26, rue de la Libération
92210 St-Cloud, France.
Tél.: 33. 1. 49. 11. 15. 50
Télex: 33. 1. 47. 71. 07. 91

Contact: CREAVISION s.a.
c/.el Berlinés 5
08006 — Barcelona (Spain)
Tel: 34-3-2094293 / 2012097
Fax: 34-3-2013444

ENRIC AROMI STUDIOS
c/. Santiago Rusinyol, 14
08310 — Argentona (Barcelona)
Spain
Tel: 34-3-7560067

282

JOHN ADAMS STUDIOS

John Adams — fashion, advertising and calendar photographer is available for commissions in his fully equipped studio in central London or on location in the UK and abroad.

156 New Cavendish Street
London W1M 7FJ
England
Tel: 071-636 3408
Fax: 071-436 7131

ADAMS PICTURE LIBRARY

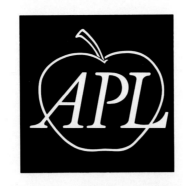

156 New Cavendish Street
London W1M 7FJ
England
Tel: 071-636 1468
Fax: 071-436 7131

Adams Picture Library has over half a million transparencies, the selected work of over 400 photographers from all over the world. Many subjects are stocked in great depth. The library is constantly being updated with new material. Adams Picture Library is conveniently situated close to the Telecom Tower in central London. Please ask for brochure.

284 MARK GATEHOUSE

18-20 St John Street
Smithfield
London EC1M 4AY
Tel: 071-251 9441
Fax: 071-490 3103

Mark works for advertising, design, editorial and marketing clients, producing photographs of people and still lives both in the studio and on location.
To produce work without delay and surcharges the studio has 24 hour lab facilities.
Amongst other clients, Mark has produced work for B.B.C., Collins Publishing, Communique, Double Exposure, I.P.C. Magazines, Wunderman Worldwide.
The photo of Caren Le Berre (International 071-487 3145) is reproduced courtesy of James Miller 081-455 0696.

Bermondsey House
163-167 Bermondsey Street
London SE1 3UW
Tel: 071 - 403 5363
Fax: 071 - 357 7054

STEPHEN PIOTROWSKI

28/29 Great Sutton Street
London EC1V 0DS
Tel: 071-253 0169
Fax: 071-251 3843

DAVE KING v

6 Charterhouse Works
Eltringham Street
London SW18 1TD
Tel: 081-874 3700
Mobile: 0860 300755

Publishing, Corporate, Advertising.
Clients Include: ACS Coffee Services, Airport Magazine, Acorn User, Bells Whiskey, Business Magazine, Coal Advisory Service, Coca Cola, Dalgety, Dorling Kindersley Publishing, Elle Magazine, Guy Salmon, Harrods, Haymarket Publishing, Jersey Royal Potatoes, Macdonald Orbis Publishing, Mac Magazine, Marshall Cavendish Publishing, Morphey Richards, Octopus Publishing, Redwood Publishing, Rank Hovis McDougall, Security Pacific, Sharwoods, Smirnoff, Tantofex.

STEVE SHIPMAN

People
Advertising and
Design

Represented by
Kathrine Maginnis
5 Kingswater Place
Battersea Church Road
London SW11 3LY
Tel: 071 978 4939
Fax: 071 978 4849

Radio Times

PAUL DUNN

Still Life
Advertising and
Design

Represented by
Kathrine Maginnis
5 Kingswater Place
Battersea Church Road
London SW11 3LY
Tel: 071 978 4939
Fax: 071 978 4849

Self Promotion

BMP DDB Needham

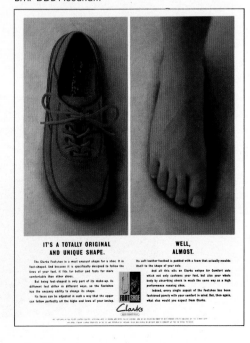

PAUL VENNING

1 Stable Yard
Danemere Street
London SW15
Tel: 0836 738 842
Fax: 081 785 7017

Represented by
Kathrine Maginnis
5 Kingswater Place
Battersea Church Road
London SW11 3LY
Tel: 071 978 4939
Fax: 071 978 4849

NEC Computers — Bell Design

Sepro Communications

DXXIII Magazine — Ludden Taylor

Electricity Privatisation — Lloyd Northover

Electricity Privatisation — Lloyd Northover

TYGER TYGER

Specialists in still life and room set photography.

Pittbrook Street
Manchester M12 6LR
Tel: 061-274 3892
Fax: 061-273 2752

PHIL BLOTT

TYGER TYGER

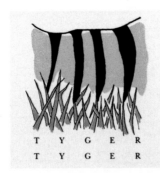

Pittbrook Street
Manchester M12 6LR
Tel: 061 -274 3892
Fax: 061 -273 2752

RICK POTTER

FRANK HOULDER

294   **BRUCE FLEMING** v

Home:
60 Wimpole Street
London W1M 7DE
Tel: 071-486 4001
Fax: 071-487 3971

Studio:
22 Hesper Mews
London SW5 0HH
Tel: 071-370 6028

Biography:
With over 30 years of experience in advertising and corporate photography, and with over 200 blue chip clients, I have the know-how, the equipment and the commitment to undertake any scale of assignment. My team and I work to exacting requirements and always meet our clients deadlines. If you have a problem to solve, an assignment to commission or would like to see more of my pictures, please call.
Credits: Makeup by Martyn Fletcher
           Production by TJ Prods

Electrolux — Sweden

Police Special Constabulary — 1991 Campaign

Gordons Gin International — Animatic "Now is the Moment"

ANTONY M. BRIGGS PHOTOGRAPHY v

Contact: Tony Briggs

199 Pullman Court
London SW2 4TA
Studio: 081-671 2508
Mobile: 0831 355688
Fax: 071-494 3133

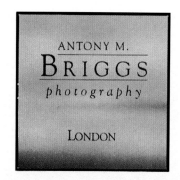

Antony has worked in commercial photography for over six years, working both in his studio in south London & on location. His work is innovative and inspiring and he has worked in a creative capacity for TV & Record Companies as well as Ad. Agencies, with Stylists, in both fashion and portrait work. Antonys work has style and he has a reputable commercial background with former clients such as Next Directory, British Telecom, Rank Xerox, BBC, Channel 4, Polydor Records, Budweiser, Mary Quant. etc.
NUJ and BETA Member.

MARK HARWOOD v

12 Clipper Court
Waterside
44-48, Wharf Road
London N1 7SF
Tel: 071-490 8787
Fax: 071-490 1009

Studio and location photography for design, publishing, corporate and advertising clients, including: British Telecom, English Heritage, Condé-Nast, Omega, Max Factor, Time-Life, Reed Publishing, Olympia & York, Tesco, Natwest, Leitz, Royal Academy of Arts, The Stock Exchange, Dunhill, Lloyds, Tissot, British Airways, Sunday Times Magazine, Bowater, GKN, Barclays, Marks and Spencer, Reuters, Kango-Wolf, Healey and Baker, Czech & Speake, Case Industries, Royal Life, Morgan Grenfell, Save and Prosper, Pentland, Debenham, Tewson & Chinnocks, Octopus Publishing, Hillier Parker, John Govett.

Currently seeking european representation, please ring for a portfolio

GEORGE LOGAN

50A Rosebery Avenue
London EC1
England
Tel: 071-833 0799/8189

Agent: Noelle Pickford
Tel: 071-584 0908

Below: Personal work
Top right: Art Director: Andrew Newton
              Client: Blue Circle
Bottom right: Art Director: Ian Lynagh
              Client: BMW

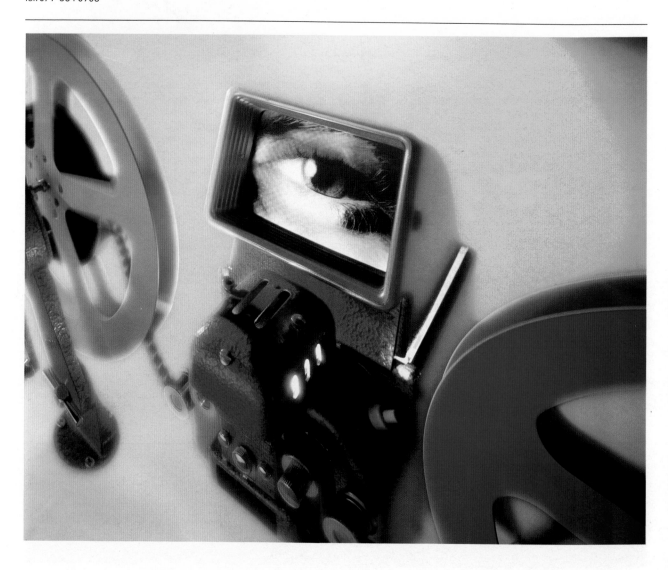

Wells Street Studios
70 Wells Street
London W1P 3RD
Tel: 071-637 8209

ADRIAN MOTT
PHOTOGRAPHY v

Mill House
Chapel Place
Rivington Street
London EC2A 3DQ
England
Tel: 071 -729 5910
Fax: 071 -729 2386

304   **KEN CHUNG v**

Ken Chung at Full Moon Productions, is based in Los Angeles and is now being represented in Europe by Bos & Co.

Specializing mainly in people, he shoots for clients as diverse as American Airlines and Lee Jeans, on both Advertising and Annual Reports, capturing a quintessentially American style.

Contact: Bos & Co.

38 Frith Street
London W1V 5TF
Tel: 071-287 8860
Fax: 071-287 0021

Lee Jeans / Fallon McElligott

Uniform / Forum Italy

Visa / Broom & Broom

Hyatt Hotels / Hill, Holiday

1 Alma Studios
32 Stratford Road
London
W8 6QF
Tel: 071 - 937 7533
Fax: 071 - 937 8285

TGV / Black and White Whisky

Lowe Howard Spink / Vauxhall

Senior King / Scandanavian Seaways Poster

DALE DURFEE

Children, people and fashion photography.
Studio and location.

The Gallery
Unit 2
38 St. Oswalds Place
London SE11 5JE
England
Tel: 071 - 735 8766

JULIAN CALDER v

2 Alma Studios
32 Stratford Road
Kensington
London W8 6QF
England
Tel: 071-937 3533

Julian Calder, who has many years experience as a reportage photographer taking pictures, now specialises in making pictures worldwide for annual reports specifically those involving portraits of people working in their environment. This year his corporate assignments have included annual reports for: Allied Lyons; Whitbread; Sainsburys; The Burton Group; Burmah Oil; BP Oil; Hawker Siddeley; British Gypsum and advertising pictures for Hilton Hotels and D.H.L. For corporate, editorial, or black & white folio call: 071-937 3533 Mobile: 0831 511640

Cocoa Warehouse — Berisfords

Hoare's Bank — The Partners

DAVID BURCH v

Specializing in food and still life photography for advertising, corporate reports, packaging, P.R., magazines and books.

11 Highbury Terrace Mews
London N5 1UT
Tel: 071-359 7435

Agent: Laura Watts
Tel: 071-485 9286
Fax: 071-485 4285

GEOFF FLETCHER v

Riverside Works
West Mills
Newbury
Berks RG14 5HY
Pager Bureau: (0345) 333111 No: 0707158
Tel: (0635) 48584
    (0635) 578430 24 hrs

Specialises in: Industrial, corporate, advertising and
architectural, location and studio
Commissions include:
Bayer UK
Quantel plc
Joint European Torus
B.R.I.T.E. Research & Development technology — Brussels
British Leyland Research & Development, Culham Labs
GLS Design: Jaguar, Oracle UK, Tektronix UK.

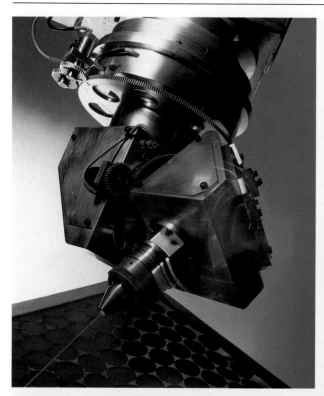

TOBI CORNEY
A.C.T.T. MEMBER

2nd Floor
38D Georgiana Street
London NW1 0EB
Tel: 071-284 2148
Radio Pager: 071-884 3344
        ID. Code: TOBY 1
Fax: 071-284 0437

Advertising, Music Business, Editorial, Film and T.V.
Please call to see the book.

Jeeves and Wooster II/Carnival Prods

Peter Donohoe/EMI

PHIL RUDGE

Contact: Lou Jessop

Dingle Dell
High Street
Whitchurch-on-Thames
Berks RG8 7EX
Tel: (0734) 845893

Advertising
Fashion
Editorial
Annual Reports
Reportage
Clients include:
Unilever, Peat Marwick McLintock, Citroen, Peugeot,
Dewe Rogerson, Haymarket Publishing, Digital.

BOS & CO. v

Contact: Mark Bostock

38 Frith Street
London W1V 5TF
Tel: 071-287 8860
Fax: 071-287 0021

Bos & Co. represents photographers based mainly in London, and is also agent for Ken Chung in Los Angeles, and Rodney Stewart in Milan and Melbourne. Each portfolio has been selected for individuality, style and professionalism. As agents, Bos & Co., run by former photographer, Mark Bostock, will handle all aspects of planning and production, and with our contacts, can organize shoots of any size, worldwide. We produce work for Design Groups and Advertising Agencies with equal enthusiasm, and fees are realistic and negotiable. Please call us if you would like to view our General Portfolio or any individual book.

KEN CHUNG

DUNCAN McNICOL

GIDEON HART

JOHN HOLLINGSHEAD

GREG BARTLEY

RODNEY STEWART

Tel: 071-833 4482

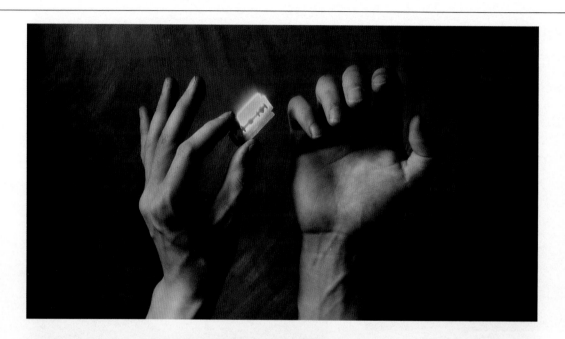

DAVID KAMPFNER v

Southern Light Studios
35A Britannia Row
London N1 8QH
Tel: 071-359 3605
Fax: 071-359 1454
Mobile: 0836 231347

Specialising in:
People
Locations
Clients include:
Abbey National, Barclays Bank, Channel Four
Rothmans, Vauxhall
Represented in London by: Christine McCarra
Tel: 071-226 4354
Pager: 081-884 3344 / Code F4028
in Paris by: Celina Walsh
Tel: 40 71 08 62

H. ROSS FELTUS

Photo-Designer BFF, BDG
Kronprinzenstr. 127
D-4000 Düsseldorf 1
Germany
Tel: 0211 / 306011
Fax: 0211 / 393398

JOHN DIETRICH

Represented by:
Brian David King
Tel: 021 - 554 7433
Fax: 021 - 554 8238

BOB KNIGHT

London
Tel: 071 - 490 0741
Mobile: 0860 681461
International:
44 - 71 - 490 - 0741

Location
Interiors
People
Travel
Corporate

For: advertising agencies
design consultants
international hotel companies
travel & leisure companies

IAN WREN

Studio & location photography at home and abroad.
Top Courtesy of Jaguar, agency Warwicks,
A.D. Keith Doherty.

321

2 Putney Road
Freemens Common
Leicester LE2 7TF
Tel: (0533) 551804
    (0836) 322720
Fax: (0533) 854617

14A Rosebery Avenue
London EC1R 4TD
Tel: 071-837 6873

Represented by: Ceri James
Tel: 071-281 2678

JON PURCELL

14 Studland Street
London W6 OJS
England
Tel: 081-748 4452
Mobile: 0860 564333

Cars, Trains, Boats, Planes....
Studio and Location.

'GIVE US A BREAK'

The colleges featured on the following pages are all affiliated to AFAEP, The Association of Fashion, Advertising and Editorial Photographers. Many of the students whose names appear in the credits will shortly be working in these areas of professional photography.

Kodak Limited is proud to have helped bring these pages into being, and the work of these students to your notice.

BOURNEMOUTH & POOLE COLLEGE OF ART & DESIGN

BARKING COLLEGE OF TECHNOLOGY

BLACKPOOL & FLYDE COLLEGE

CHELTENHAM & GLOUCESTER COLLEGE

CLEVELAND COLLEGE OF ART & DESIGN

HARROW COLLEGE

KINGSWAY COLLEGE

KENT INSTITUTE OF ART & DESIGN

MANCHESTER POLYTECHNIC

NAPIER COLLEGE

PLYMOUTH COLLEGE OF ART

SALISBURY COLLEGE OF ART

SOUTHAMPTON INTITUTE

STAFFORDSHIRE POLYTECHNIC

STOCKPORT COLLEGE OF TECHNOLOGY

NEWCASTLE UPON TYNE COLLEGE

WATFORD COLLEGE

WEST GLAMORGAN INSTITUTE

BOURNEMOUTH & POOLE COLLEGE OF ART & DESIGN

Contact: Sylvia Barnes

Head of School: Photography
Wallisdown
Poole
Dorset BH12 5HH
Tel: 0202 533011 ext. 246
Fax: 0202 537729

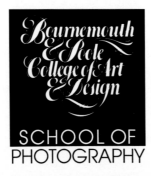
326

LESTER PO FUN LEE

BARKING COLLEGE OF TECHNOLOGY

Contact: Ed Kinge

Charlecote Annexe
Charlecote Road
Dagenham
Essex RM8 3LD
Tel: 081-595 3233/4

The photographs shown are by students on the BTEC National Diploma course in Photography, which offers a broad based education in the application of creative professional photography. Many students progress to HND or Degree courses.

The College also offers City & Guilds 747, which allows students to study professional photography competences.

JOEL PORTER

SIMON SANDYS

JEREMY WILKINSON

BEN JOSEPH

BLACKPOOL AND THE FYLDE COLLEGE v

What a year! We've had more books called for than ever. This means I can't show you the client list because it's too big to fit in! The students find it very encouraging that you feel they're producing the creative solutions you're looking for. Thanks for the vote of confidence.

Contact: Geoff Clark

Tel: 0253 293071 ext. 254
Fax: 0253 752209

MICHAEL LEWIS

JAMES STAFFORD

PHILIP ARNOULD

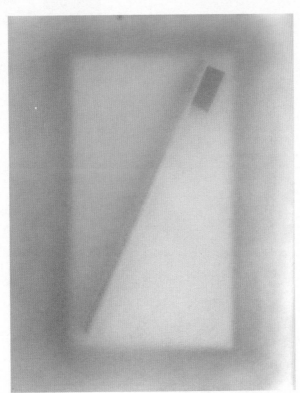

NEIL BLAKE

ROB ASHTON

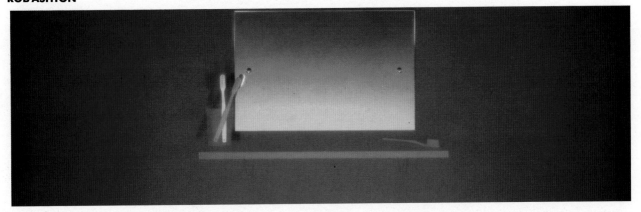

TIM PARR

RICHARD MANKI

DAVE HARWOOD

LYNDA BUSSEY

BEN WILSON

DAMON MEREDITH

JOANNE KENNILS

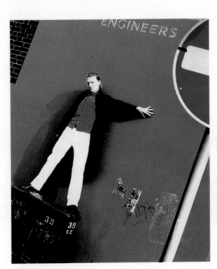

JUSTIN QUICK

PETER MARCHETTI

CHELTENHAM & GLOUCESTER COLLEGE

School of Photography
Media Centre
Brunswick Road
Gloucester GL1 1HS
England

Tel: (0452) 426619

Cheltenham & Gloucester College offers a B/TEC Higher National Diploma in photography. The course is aimed at continuing the education and training of students committed to a career in editorial and advertising photography. Studio, location, video and overseas projects are designed to realise the students' creative potential whilst teaching the technical and professional skills needed in their chosen career. Periods of work release are a vital part of the course, often proving helpful in maintaining the college's strong record of employment.

DOMINI PETT

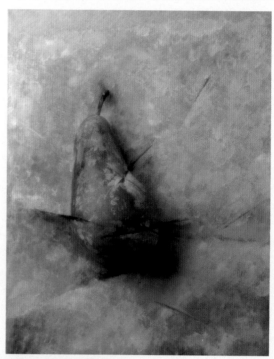

CHRISTIAN MCGOWAN

PHILLIP JAMES

CLEVELAND COLLEGE OF ART & DESIGN v

Contact: Alan Hampson

Cleveland College of Art & Design
Green Lane
Linthorpe
Middlesbrough
Cleveland TS5 7RJ
Tel: (0642) 821441
Fax: (0642) 823441

CLEVELAND
COLLEGE OF
ART & DESIGN

The Department of Design Studies offers two courses:
BTEC Higher National Diploma in Design, with a
specialist option in Photography.
BTEC National Diploma in Design (Photography, Film
& Television).
The courses already have a national reputation
attracting students from the length and breadth of the
Country. We have excellent employment records and an
increasing number of Awards from major Competitions.

CLAIRE MONK

NEIL BLACKBURN

PCL HARROW COLLEGE

Contact: Duncan Backhouse

BA(HONS) Photography Film & Video
Watford Road
Northwick Park
Harrow HA1 3TP
Tel: 071-911 5000

CARLOS ECHAVARRIA

ALISON CURRIE

ALYSON SIMMONS

KINGSWAY COLLEGE

For more information please contact:
Mac Campeanu
Visual Arts Unit
Photography Section
Sans Walk
London EC1R 0AS
England
Tel: 071-278 0541

The section offers a broad range of courses in photography and photographic laboratory work. The pictures shown here are by students on our B/TEC National Diploma Course in Photography and Photographic Laboratory Practice. This two year full-time course is most appropriate for students who either wish to progress to Higher Education, or find work in a professional laboratory. The National Diploma course offers a broadly based programme which concentrates on the craft and technical skills involved in professional photographic practice.

VOTU ERUOTOR

OSMAN DEEN

KENT INSTITUTE OF ART & DESIGN

Contact: George Wattson

Rochester-upon-Medway College
Fort Pitt
Rochester
Kent ME1 1DZ
England
Tel: (0634) 830022 ext: 273

High National Diploma in Advertising and Editorial Photography.
The close proximity to London, well established contacts with Advertising and Editorial Photographers is reflected in both students' Industrial Release and their immediate post college professional career.
The 'illustrative' photograph adjacent by Chris Pert was part of a college project.
Chris also undertook a major series of photographs in Eastern Europe during his final year (1990).

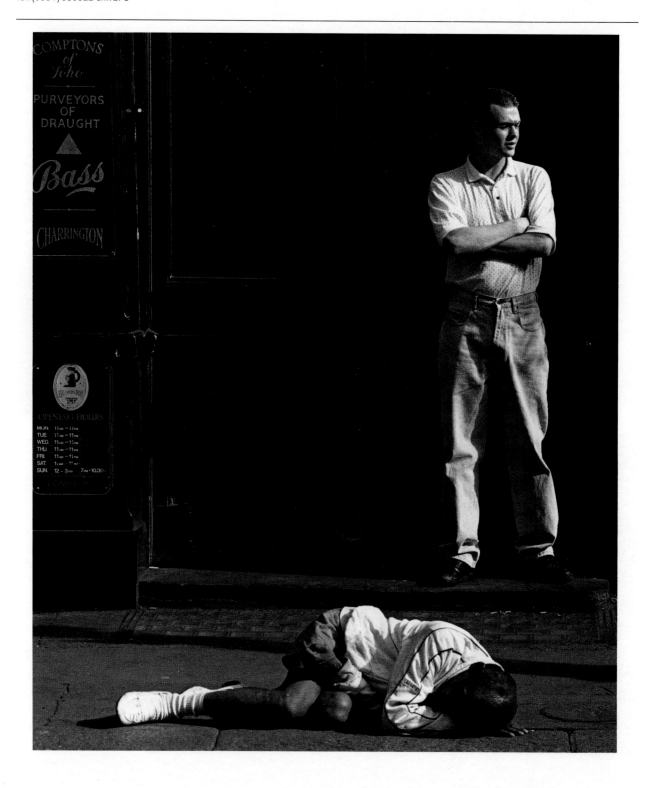

NEWCASTLE COLLEGE

Contact: Bill Jenkins

School of Art and Design
Rye Hill
Newcastle-upon-Tyne
NE4 7SA
England
Tel: 091-273 8866

Newcastle College offer a BTEC Higher National Diploma in photography and audio visual media with specialist options in advertising and editorial photography, commercial photography and audio visual media. Housed in a new purpose built building the School of Art and Design lies close to the city centre which hosts many attractions for young people.

MARTIN MALLETT

JONATHAN BENNETT

MANCHESTER POLYTECHNIC

Faculty of Art and Design
Cavendish Street
Manchester M15 6BR
Tel: 061-247 1302/3/4
Fax: 061-236 0820

Photography — BA (Hons)
Design for Commucication
Media

Photo by Alan Jones
Tel: 061-226 0155

NAPIER POLYTECHNIC

The BA Photography course at Napier Polytechnic
is one of the few Degree programmes where
photography is studied within a professional context.
The course also covers other visual media including film,
video, slide/tape and graphic design besides
Communication, Historical and Business Studies.

61 Marchmont Road
Edinburgh EH9 1HU
Scotland
Tel: 031 - 444 2266
Fax: 031 - 455 7209

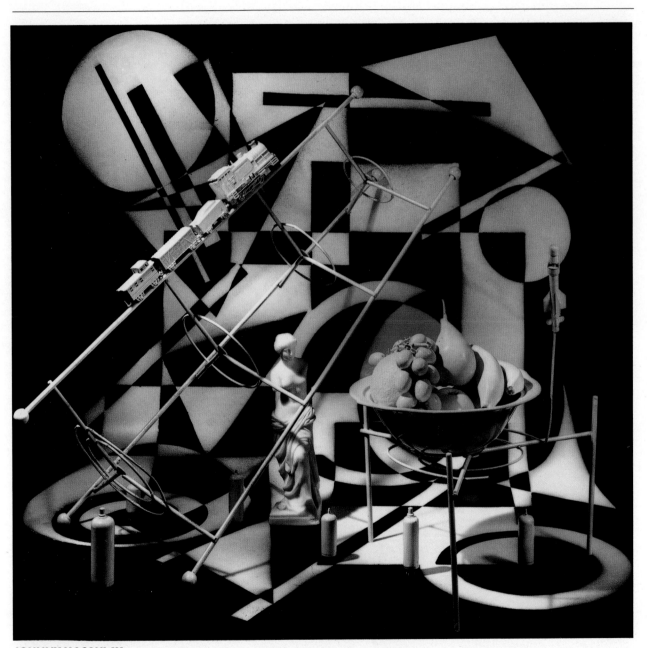

JOHNNY MACAULAY

SALISBURY COLLEGE OF ART & DESIGN

Tomorrow's Image Makers
Department of Photography
Film & Television
Southampton Road, Salisbury
Wiltshire SP1 2PP
England
Tel: (0722) 326122
Fax: (0722) 331972

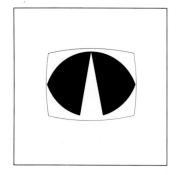

Salisbury College of Art & Design's Department of Photography is educating Tomorrow's Image Makers. The Department's reputation within the visual communication industry is based upon its ability to produce skilled and motivated graduates. Such reputations are hard won and are the result of years spent maintaining and, indeed, raising standards. The courses on offer at Salisbury occupy a three-year period of full-time education. Specialist facilities in video, film and tape/slide production exist alongside stills-based studios.

Tony Gilbert *Advertising contact 0275 393381*

Kin Ho *Fashion contact College*

Jonathan Rapley *Fashion contact College*

John Beynon *Advertising contact College*

Richard Gleed *People & Advertising contact College*

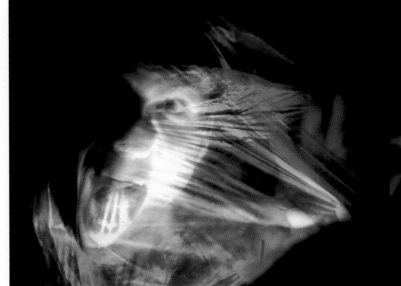

rian Lyon *Advertising contact College*

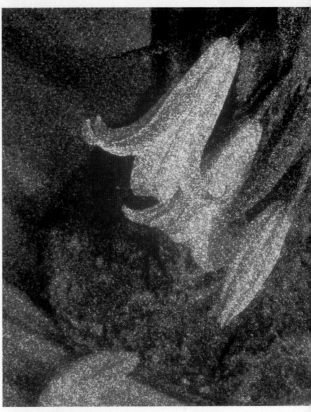

Colin Hoskins *Travel 0373 62992*
(Worlds View, Nyanga, ZIMBABWE)

Sandra Lambell *Advertising contact College*

PLYMOUTH COLLEGE OF ART AND DESIGN, PHOTOGRAPHY, FILM AND TELEVISION

Tavistock Place
Plymouth
Devon PL4 8AT
England
Tel: (0752) 385987
Fax: (0752) 385972

The College offers BTEC National Diploma in Photography; BTEC Higher National Diploma in Photography, Film and Television; and an Advanced Diploma in Photography Film and Television leading to the British Institute of Professional Photography P.Q.E. The Higher National Diploma course allows students to specialise in one of three options, Photography; Combined Media; Film and Television, whilst the P.Q.E offers students the opportunity to follow a specialised course of study.

SUKI DHANDA

TUDOR MORGAN-OWEN

MATTHEW ROWE

SALLY-ANN NORMAN

LYNNE MORGAN

NIGEL HANCOCK

MARIA MOORE

VICKY CORNELL

GRAHAM COOPER-HOLMES

CRAIG JUDD

ALUN BULL

SIMON GREEN

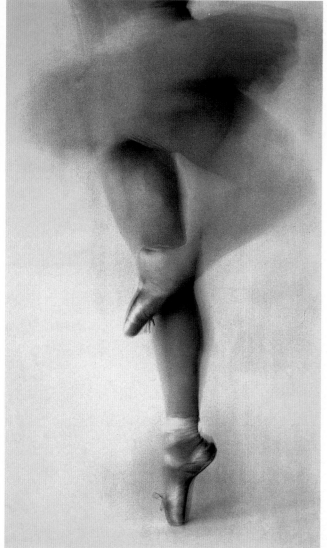

SOUTHAMPTON INSTITUTE OF HIGHER EDUCATION

Design Division
East Park Terrace
Southampton
Hampshire SO9 4WW
England
Tel: (0703) 229381

Southampton Campus

The Design Division offers Courses in Fashion, Graphics, Industrial Design and Fine Art, all students study Photography, using their creative skills as Designers attaining a high degree of expertise and professional ability. The aquisition of Apple Macintosh II CX terminals, students are beginning to use these computers to retouch and manipulate their images. The Division's accommodation looks out on pleasant parkland in the very heart of the city with easy access via the M3 and M27 Motorways, Intercity Rail Links and into Europe by air from Eastleigh Airport and Continental Ferry Ports.

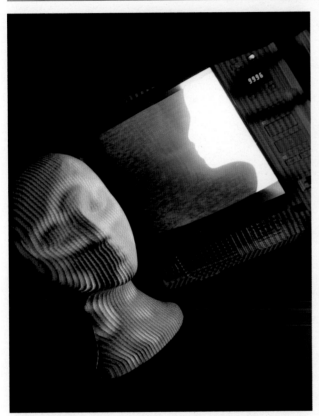

ROGER JONES

MIRANDA EVANS

JEETENDRA TAILOR

TERRY GOULDING

STAFFORDSHIRE POLYTECHNIC

College Road
Stoke-on-Trent ST4 2DE
England
Tel: (0782) 744531
Fax: (0782) 744035

Photography is one of the areas of specialisation within the BA(Hons) design course, one of the largest in Britain. We aim to educate and encourage students to communicate imaginatively and with effect, using photography in its broadest applications.

Students also have the opportunity to extend their experience and abilities into additional design disciplines offered on the course, involving graphics, audio visual and computer aided design. Graduates enter a wide range of employment, from film production, art direction, to the whole spectrum of photographic practice.

Azerbaijan 1990

Stoke

STOCKPORT COLLEGE OF FURTHER & HIGHER EDUCATION

Faculty of Design
Wellington Road South
Stockport
Cheshire SK1 3UQ
England
Tel: 061-474 3711
(photography)

Course director: Barry Ainsworth
BTEC National Diploma in Photography. A broad based course but with an emphasis towards advertising and editorial/social documentary photography.
Its aim is to produce thinking photographers with the skills, enthusiasm and commitment necessary to succeed.

GREG GOODWIN

ALEX LIVESEY

NICOLE SCHROEDER

ALISON GORVIN

WATFORD COLLEGE

Department of Printing and Packaging
Water Lane, Watford
Herts WD1 2NN

Photography Section:
Ron Southwell, Bob Irons,
Alistair Lamb, David Whittington-Jones
Tel: (0923) 57508 Extn. 197
Fax: (0923) 211536

The Photographic Courses at Watford College have been designed to develop the technical and creative skills of would be professional photographers. The specific aims are to encourage young people to understand, interpret and operate photographically in conjuction with the other elements of design used in the production of visual communication material.
It is a learning environment in which the full implications of professional, technical and creative elements of the photographic industry are given major emphasis.

COLIN DUTTON *081-950 1814*

WARREN HUNT *0923 778294*

ALISON STEVENS *0908 606619*

PETER 'RED' BARRON

WEST GLAMORGAN INSTITUTE OF HIGHER EDUCATION

Photography Department
Townhill Road
Swansea SA2 0UT
Wales
Tel: (0792) 203482

Course Director: David Pitt ext. 2225
Tutors: Suzanne Greenslade ext. 2218
               Reggie Tucker ext. 2208

The course at Swansea encourages and stimulates work of a highly creative nature within a professional context, specialising in Advertising, Industrial and Editorial photography, allowing the student a broad base of experience and expertise.
The Brecon Beacons, Gower Peninsula and urban and industrial developments provide students with a unique visual resource.

ANDY MACDONALD KENEALY

SAM SCOTT-HUNTER

BRITISH ASSOCIATION OF PICTURE LIBRARIES AND AGENCIES

13 Woodberry Crescent
Muswell Hill
London N10 1PJ
Telephone: 081 444 7913
Fax: 081 883 9215

The 1990/91 Directory of the British Association of Picture Libraries and Agencies gives access to over 200 million pictures from over two hundred and seventy libraries and agencies, some very large and some very small. A description of each member library with details of how to make contact, is followed by a subject index of specialist collections to enable users to discover easily, which library or agency holds the type of material required.

Using this Directory

Quantity

Under each entry in the alphabeticl listings is a line giving additional information which may be of some use to picture users. The first item, Quantity, gives some idea of the size of each library; under 10,000 images*, 10,000-75,000 images**, 75,000-250,000 images *** and over 250,000 images **** The size of a library is no indication of the quality of the collection and for specialist material a small library may be the only source.

A.M. Photo Agency and Colour Library

40 Croft Close, Rowton, Chester, Cheshire CH3 7QQ
Tel: 0244 332060
Contact: Michael Reed

A recently formed and rapidly expanding general colour library stocking 35mm and medium format transparencies from photographers based mainly in the UK and featuring the North-West of England and North Wales. Leisure and sporting activities include contemporary Rugby League and motor sports. We have sections on natural history, animals, birds, flowers, travel and transport.
Quantity Format S/M Colour C-D B/W**

A-Z Botanical Collection Ltd

Bedwell Lodge, Cucumber Lane, Essendon, Hatfield, Hertfordshire AL9 6JB
Tel: 0707 49091
Contact: Jeremy Finlay
Fax: 0707 46613

A wide ranging and continually expanding specialist photo library of 35mm and medium format transparencies of world-wide plant life. Flowers, trees, shrubs, vegetables, crops, gardens and garden features. Horticulture and agriculture. Fruit, fungi, lichens and wild flowers. Many overseas contributors.
Quantity* Format S/M Colour C-D B/W**

AA Photo Library

Fanum House, Basingstoke, Hants RG21 2EA
Tel: 0256 491588
Contact: Mrs W Voysey
Fax: 0256 22575

An extensive collection mainly of colour transparencies 35mm and medium format from England, Scotland and Wales, of Britain and its landscape, commissioned by the Automobile Association's Publication Division. We cover towns, villages and places of interest and are strong on lesser known areas of the UK.
Quantity Format S/M Colour D**

Ace Photo Agency

22 Maddox Street, Mayfair, London W1R 9PG
Tel: 071 629 0303
Contact: John Panton
Fax: 071 495 6100

In-depth colour files on people and life-styles, business, industry, technology, sports, skies and sunsets, beaches, glamour, animals, abstracts, textures, still-life, special effects, transport, UK and world travel, music and arts, celebrities, natural history, moods and concepts, plus many more. Pin-reg AV sequences also available. Formats 35mm to 10 x 8, mostly originals. Regular stock shoots organised by Ace to anticipate future demand. Worldwide network of photographers and sub-agents. Bulk discounts by negotiation. Central London location —visits are most welcome. Deluxe stock catalogues (Vols 2 & 3), featuring over 2,250 images, available free on application. Office hours 9.30 to 6.00. Assignment work in own studios. Stock illustrations also available.
Quantity** Format S/M/L Colour D Illustration**

Action Images Sports Picture Library

12 Cambridge Terrace, Bury Street West, London N9 9JJ
Tel: 081 364 1010
Contact: David Jacobs
Fax: 081 364 0040

Action images supplies worldwide sports photo services for editorial, TV, advertising, etc. Colour and b/w library with half a million images on file. Computerised retrieval service and immediate dispatch. File includes personalities in sport, major events and leisure activities. Picture researchers welcome. Commissions undertaken.
Quantity** Format M Colour B/C/D B/W**

Action Plus Photographic

54/58 Tanner Street, London SE1 3LL
Tel: 071 403 1558
Contact: Jane Plummer
Fax: 071 403 1526
Telex: 8951182 GECOMS G

An extensive and constantly expanding library of professional and amateur sports, leisure and action images. Colour and b/w, suitable for editorial and commercial use. Imaginative coverage of over 100 international sports and leisure activities. Original photographic commissions undertaken worldwide by our British and American based photographers. Fast and friendly service for visitors and telephone callers.
Quantity** Format S Colour D B/W**

Adams Picture Library
156 New Cavendish Street, London W1M 7FJ
Tel: 071 636 1468
Contact: Carol White
Fax: 071 436 7131

Conveniently situated in Central London in the shadow of the Telecom Tower, Adams Picture Library houses some 500,000 transparencies in various formats, selected from the work of over 400 photographers. To satisfy the ever-increasing visual needs of commerce and professional communicators, APL is constantly developing its worldwide sources, adding new material to the wide range of subjects and categories in its collection including computer graphics. This and a fast, efficient service make APL first call to those seeking top quality shots ASAP. Please ask for a brochure.
Quantity**** Formats S/M/L Colour D

The Advertising Archives
45 Lyndale Avenue, London NW2 2QB
Tel: 071 837 6743/071 435 6540
Contact: Suzanne Viner
Fax: 071 837 8701

A unique picture library specialising in 20th Century American and British magazines, magazine cover illustration and advertising. Over 1 million images categorised and cross-referenced for easy access. Clients can visit by appointment or alternatively we research projects for you and present a selection of relevant material. Extensive collection of Norman Rockwell and Leyendecker illustrations. Clients include advertising agencies, art and design studios, fashion design groups, interior designers, retail display departments, publishers and private collectors. An inspiration source for a variety of creative fields.
Quantity**** Illustration

AFP and EPA (Agence-France Presse and European Pressphoto Agency)
Available from Popperfoto
24 Bride Lane, Fleet St., London EC4Y 8DR
Tel: 071 353 9665/6
Contact: Liz Moore
Fax: 071 936 2153
Telex: 8814206 POPPER G

Daily news coverage on international events. B/W pictures are transmitted, but good quality 35mm colour transparencies are also available. B/W commences August 1989 and colour from April 1990. Subjects cover personalities, Royalty, crime, politics, demonstrations and sport, including the 1990 World Cup. European current affairs are especially well covered as well as worldwide events.
Quantity**** Format S Colour D B/W

Malcolm Aird Associates
Falcon House, 12/14 Swan Street, Boxford, Colchester,
Essex CO6 5NZ
Tel: 0787 210111
Contact: Robert Estall
Fax: 0787 211440

Landscapes, cities, towns and villages of Britain. Industry, crafts and people at work. Modern commercial aircraft and new transport. All material supplied as originals.
Quantity** Format S/M Colour C-D

Airpic (Industrial) Ltd
Lea Industrial Estate, Lower Luton Road, Harpenden,
Hertfordshire AL5 5EQ
Tel: 0582 768167/461700
Contact: Neale Bryant
Fax: 0582 761549

A computerised aerial photographic library containing locations throughout the UK. Composed mainly of obliques, the library dates back 20 years though over 100,000 shots have been taken since 1987. 'The County Collection' consists of villages, towns, city centres and suburbs, industrial sites and buildings. Photographs are categorised and can be accessed on the computer either by name or geographical location. 'The Classic Collection', is a smaller, specific library of sites of particular regional and national interest, famous landmarks, castles, buildings, monuments and stadiums, etc. For the right shot, an all year commissioned service exists throughout the UK and parts of Europe.
Quantity*** Format M Colour C-D

Alba Pictures
The Sutors, 28 Broadstone Park, Inverness, Highland IV2 3LA
Tel: 0463 233717
Contact: Ken Mac Taggart

Specialist in Scottish Highlands and Islands, world travel and mountaineering. Scottish coverage of landscape, mountains, coasts, islands, towns, castles, ancient monuments. Foreign coverage of scenery, cities, holidays and property in about 40 countries and 15 American States. Mountaineering, hill walking, rock and snow climbing coverage of Scotland, Wales, Lake District, Alps, other Europe, the Arctic, Mexico, North America. Geology and land forms including volcanoes, glaciers, moraines, erosion, rivers, beaches. General landscapes of mist, sunsets, snow, forests, breakers. Spacecraft, space shuttle and moon flights. Mostly 35mm transparencies, some b/w prints.
Quantity* Format S Colour C-D

Bryan and Cherry Alexander Photography
Higher Cottage, Manston, Sturminster Newton,
Dorset DT10 1EZ.
Tel: 0258 73006
Contact: Cherry Alexander
Fax: 0747 51474

The Arctic is our speciality and for twenty years we have recorded in great detail the lifestyles of its indigenous peoples and the technology that is changing their lives and their land. Polar bears, walrus and other Arctic wildlife are well covered. We are also constantly adding to our file on British fieldsports. Because of our assignment work for magazines we have in depth coverage on subjects as diverse as mazes and yak herders. Same day service if you ask in time. Red Star is close by.
Quantity*** Format S Colour C-D

All-Sport (U.K.) Ltd.
All-Sport House, 3 Greenlea Park, Prince Georges Road,
London SW19 2JD.
Tel: 081 685 1010
Contact: Adrian Murrell
Fax: 081 648 5240
Telex: 8955022 ASPORT G

The world's largest specialist sports library, covering 130 different sports and all the world's top sports personalities. 35mm colour transparencies available for editorial and commercial use. Represented in 27 countries worldwide. Featuring the work of Tony Duffy, Steve Powell, Adrian Murrell, Dave Cannon, Bob Martin, Mike Powell, Simon Bruty, Russell Cheyne, Pascal Rondeau, Ben Radford, Dan Smith. Also available is the archive from the British Olympic Association including b/w material from the end of the 19th Century to the present. Large in-house studio facility.
Quantity**** Format S Colour B-C-D B/W

Chris Allan Aviation Library
21-22 St Albans Place, Upper Street, Islington, London N1 0NX
Tel: 071 226 1508
Contact: Anna Kafetz
Fax: 071 359 8523
Telex: 269406 Camera G

This library specialises in pictures from the world's finest aviation photographers who are based in the UK, the Far East and the USA. We offer a collection of colour transparencies covering all significant combat aircraft in service in the UK, North America ad Asia, including rare air shots of modern, fast jets. A comprehensive selection of civil aircraft is available, including jets, propeller and helicopters, plus a selection of unique shots of the Red Arrows Display Team. Much of the material has been shot on medium format resulting in an increase in quality. The collection is continually updated and offes a fast, efficient service.
Quantity* Format S/M Colour D

Ancient Art & Architecture Collection
6 Kenton Road, Harrow-on-the-Hill, London HA1 2BL
Tel: 081 422 1214
Contact: The Librarian
Fax: 081 426 9479

Dramatic and imformative worldwide images from our computerised photo library of pictures in colour and b/w covering travel, painting, sculpture, engraving and woodcuts, stained glass, wood and stone carving, enamels, jewellery, tapestries, mosaics, weapons, archaeology, architecture including castles, temples, chateaux, palaces, houses, pyramids, tombs, megaliths, industrial archaeology, geographical and historical material from pre-history to the present.
Quantity**** Format S/M/L Colour B-C-D B/W Illustration

Heather Angel/Biofotos
Highways, 6 Vicarage Hill, Farnham, Surrey GU9 8HJ
Tel: 0252 716700
Contact: Heather Angel
Fax: 0252 727464

Comprehensive expanding library of original transparencies, 35mm and medium format and some b/w. Worldwide wildlife, natural history, sea and landscapes, underwater, plants, animals, close-up and geological subjects. Associated photographers include Brian Rogers' tropical rain forest fauna and flora. Amphibians, birds, insects, pond and marine life, fish, fossils, reptiles, mammals, seaweeds, fungi, lichens, mosses, ferns, flowers, gardens, whales, tree from Africa, Asia (notably China), Australia, South America and USA. Commissions undertaken. Detailed subject catalogue available on request.
Quantity**** Format S/M Colour C-D B/W

Animal Photography Ltd
4 Marylebone Mews, New Cavendish Street, London W1M 7LF
Tel: 071 935 0503
Contact: John Thompson

Colour and b/w photographs of most breeds of horses and dogs. Large selection of cats. Galapagos Islands, animals in Zoos, some East African animals and French subjects. Commissions undertaken.
Quantity** Format S/M Colour B-C-D B/W

Aquarius Picture Library
PO Box 5, Hastings, East Sussex TN34 1HR
Tel: 0424 721196
Contact: Gilbert Gibson
Fax: 0424 717704

Initially formed as an extention of Aquarius Literary Agency, the library, with nearly 1 million images in colour and b/w, operates as a seperate entity supplying publishing, television and advertising agencies with a specialised service. Stills from films dating from the start of the century to the present with movie colour in 10 ×8 as well as candids. Opera, ballet, TV and pop. Requests by phone dispatched same day. Over 4,000 personalities represented with new images added every week. Collection includes Hollywood Press Service.
Quantity**** Format S/M/L/ Colour A-B-C-D B/W

Aquila Photographics Ltd
PO Box 1, Haydon House, Ascester Road, Studley,
Warwickshire B80 7AN
Tel: 052785 2357
Contact: Alan Richards
Fax: 052785 7507

We cover the whole specturm of natural history from liverworts and mosses through to flowers, insects, amphibia, reptiles, birds and mammals. We have colour and b/w of many forms of British and European wildlife and a good coverage of many other parts of the world, especially North America, Africa and Australia. Birds are our speciality on which subject we can alo advise and help if required.
Quantity*** Format S/M Colour C-D B/W

Arcaid
The Factory, Rear of 2 Acre Road, Kingston-on-Thames,
Surrey KT2 6EF
Tel: 081 546 4352
Contact: Lynne Bryant
Fax: 081 541 5230

Arcaid's architectural and interior design picture library incorporates material from Richard Bryant, Richard Einzig, Lucinda Lambton and other leading architectual photographers. The collection covers international subjects and includes an extensive collection on Britain. Historic and contemporary subjects have been photographed during the last twenty years and encompass civic, residential and commercial architecture, interior and garden design. Coverage ranges from a single image to comprehensive series. Commissions undertaken. Visitors welcome by appointment.
Quantity** Format S/M/L Colour B-C-D B/W

Architectural Association Slide Library
36 Bedford Square, London WC1B 3ES
Tel: 071 636 0974
Contact: Valerie Bennett

A collection of architectural images built up since the end of the 19th Century. 65,000 35mm colour transparencies and some b/w divided broadly into historical and 20th Century building. Other areas covered include town planning, gardens and landscape. As well as the colour transparencies in the main collection, the library has an archive of b/w negatives and prints dating from the 1920's and some lantern slides.
Quantity*** Format S/M Colour A-B-C-D B/W

Ardea London Ltd
35 Brodrick Road, London SW17 7DX
Tel: 081 672 2067
Contact: Su Gooders
Fax: 081 672 8787
Telex: 896691 TLX1RG
        prefix Ardeaphotos

A specialist natural history photographic library with over 100,000 original transparencies of animals, birds, plants, fish, insects and reptiles from all over the world. Most of the creatures have been taken wild and free in their natural habitat but we also have cats, dogs and horses; in fact, everything to do with the natural world. Many of our contributors live and work in wild, remote areas, providing desert sands, Antarctic ice cliffs, tropical rainforests and Aborigines as well as farming, pollution, conservation, sunsets and scenery. Colour and b/w.
Quantity*** Format S/M/L Colour C-D B/W

Art Directors Photo Library
Image House, 86 Haverstock Hill, London NW3 2BD
Tel: 071 485 9325/071 267 6930
Contact: David Harding
Fax: 071 485 7776

A constantly expanding library of over a quarter million
transparencies from top international photographers. Includes
backgrounds for advertising, incorporating many of the best lensmen
of US *National Geographic Magazine*. Computer graphics, Hi-Tech,
industry and business, space, personalities, families, couples, life-style,
travel, landscapes, skies, medicine, food and drink, entertainment,
fashion, faces, animals, science, flowers, nature, vintage and modern
cars and an outstanding quality and depth of coverage on USA,
Europe, Asia, Africa, and the Tropics. Free catalogue on request.
Quantity**** Format S/M Colour C-D

Art Resource Illustration Library
28 Shelton Street, London WC2H 9JN
Tel: 071 240 1447
contact: Sue Cowley
Fax: 071 836 0199

High quality illustrations produced by well known illustrators at a
fraction of the cost of commissioned prices. The library has over 2,000
images which are constantly being added to, covering everything
from abstract to still-life, animals to architecture, sport to science
fiction, people and travel. Styles vary from ultra realistic to highly
stylised. All contributors work in the field of advertising and their
material is of the highest quality. We are one of the leading suppliers
of images to poster, greeting cards and jigsaw companies.
Commissions undertaken.
Quantity* Format S Illustration

Artbank International
8 Woodcroft Avenue, London NW7 2AG
Tel: 081 906 2288
Contact: Rick Goodale
Fax: 081 906 2289

Artbank is an international stock illustration library, licensing
reproduction rights to the existing works of many of the world's most
renowned illustrators for use in advertising, calendars, packaging,
publicity, stationery, etc. All images are on 5 ×4 format transparencies
and cover a wide range of subject matter from everyday objects to
science fiction, astrology, mythology, fantasy, etc. Where else can you
find mermaids, unicorns and centaurs? Artbank also represents the
European interest of a Japanese agency, thus giving access to a
further 40,000 works of art. Many of our artists are available for
commissioned work.
Quantity** Format L Illustration

Aspect Picture Library Ltd
40 Rostrevor Road, London SW6 5AD
Tel: 071 736 1998/731 7362
Contact: Derek Bayes
Fax: 071 731 7362
Telex: 934999 TXLINK G
    quoting MBX 219994671

Specialising in reportage features and essays around the world.
Covering countries, events, industry, travel. An extensive stock file of
colour photographes suitable for advertising, audio-visual, books,
brochures, company reports, calendars, magazines, packaging and
posters. Large files on art, paintings, space, China, Middle East.
Colour and b/w.
Quantity*** Format S/M/L Colour C-D B/W Illustration

Audio Visual Services St Mary's Hospital Medical School
Norfolk Place, Paddington, London W2 1PG
Tel: 071 725 1739
Contact: Miss B Tallon
Fax: 071 724 7349

This library, established in 1948 and regularly updated, contains
approximately 35,000 colour and b/w transparencies of medical
conditions, some now very rare. Also pictures allied to medicine, the
best of which have been incorporated into the **National Medical
Slide Bank** qv. Material is available to bona fide borrowers only
and is in constant demand from publishers and TV. Viewing by
appointment only. Pleast telephone to enquire about specific pictures
or to request photographs to be taken.
Quantity** Format S/M Colour A-B-C-D B/W

Autograph
Unit 223 Bon Marche Building, 444 Brixton Road, London SW9 8EJ
Tel: 071 737 5865

An association of non-European photographers based in the UK with
international links. Constantly expanding library in colour and b/w,
concentrating on issues around race, culture, education, politics,
gender, sexuality in the UK and other countries including Central and
North America, South Asia, the Caribbean, Africa. Commissions
undertaken. Visitors by appointment. Consultant — Martin Slavin.
Quantity** Format S/M Colour D B/W

Aviation Photographs International
15 Downs View Road, Swindon, Wilts SN3 1NS
Tel: 0793 497179
Contact: Jeremy Flack
Fax: 0739 497179

An extensive collection of aviation photographs mainly in colour.
Included are many associated subjects including internal views,
airport buildings, radar and weapons as well as views from aircraft.
Both civil and military subjects are covered and the collection is
expanding to include ships and vehicles. Subjects are catalogued on
computer giving a comprehensive and easy cross-reference facility.
We are able to assist with editorial content and accept commissions
for photography and additional picture research if required.
Quantity*** Format S Colour B-C-D

The Aviation Picture Library
35 Kingsley Avenue, West Ealing, London W13 0EQ
Tel: 081 566 7712
Mobile: 0860 292661
Contact: Austin J. Brown
Fax: 081 566 7714

A specialised source of over 100,000 original aviation transparencies
covering all aspects of the industry with an increasing bias towards
dynamic shots of aircraft. The collection consists of atmospheric views
from the gound and in the air, high and low altitude obliques of
Europe, Africa, the Caribbean and the USA and travel photographs
from these areas. We are an active photographic unit specialising in
air-to-air commissions for commercial operators and air-to-ground
obliques for land development. Architectural photography of modern
buildings and town planning, is available through the library. Some
archival material available. From contacts, almost anything can be
found.
Quantity*** Format S/M Colour C-D B/W

Aviemore Photographic
Main Road, Aviemore, Highland PH22 1RH
Tel: 0479 810371
Contact: Stewart Grant
Fax: 0479 811351

Scotland in summer and winter. Winter sports, tourism, landscapes
and mood shots. Our proximity to the centre of the Scottish winter
sports area has provided us with a large selection of skiing and
curling. Developing collection on the Scotch Whisky industry. Colour
and b/w, 35mm and medium format.
Quantity* Format S/M Colour C-D

Clive Barda
50 Agate Road, London W6 0AH
Tel: 081 741 0805
Contact: Clive Barda
Fax: 081 563 0538
Telex: 291829 BARDA

A personal archive in colour, 35mm and medium format and b/w covering all aspects of classical music and opera. Conductors, orchestras, instrumentalists, recording studios, sections of the orchestra, concerts and a wide range of costume stage shots of operas, opera singers and operatic occasions. Also interiors and exteriors of famous opera houses and concert halls in Britain and Europe. The collection is now expanding to cover stage musicals and theatre.
Quantity**** Format S/M Colour C-D B/W

Barnaby's Picture Library
19 Rathbone Street, London W1P 1AF
Tel: 071 636 6128/9
Contact: Mary Buckland
Fax: 071 637 4317

One of London's oldest established agencies with a stock of over 3 million colour and b/w pictures, all formats, embracing a wide variety of subjects ranging from nature views to transport, trains, aircraft, maritime, industry and oil, varied historical subjects and an extensive collection on Hitler. A network of photographers over the British Isles and abroad can be called upon for instant commissions.
Quantity**** Format S/M/L Colour A-B-C-D B/W

Bart's Medical Picture Library
Medical Illustration, St Bartholomew's Hospital, West Smithfield, London EC1A 7BE
Tel: 071 601 8080/81
Contact: Maureen Doyle
Fax: 071 796 3753

Possibly the longest pedigree of any medical illustration department in the UK. Our huge resource has appreciated in teaching, illustrative and historical value and is drawn on by authors, picture researchers from lay, medical and scientific journals and text book publishers and TV and other media property buyers. Scene setting pictures provide editors with shots to inject interest into news items. Reference shots for dramas and documentaries to guide simulation of injury or disease, for the accurate replication of equipment and uniforms or backgrounds for sets. Historical collection of personailities in medicine and past hospital scenes. Commissions undertaken.
Quantity** Format S/M Colour A-B-C-D B/W Illustration

James Bartholomew Photography
55 Mount Road, New Malden, Surrey KT3 3JY
Tel: 081 942 5287
Contact: James Bartholomew

James Bartholomew Photography is concerned foremost with representing London in all its forms. We hold an exclusive and wide stock of the Tower of London, Kew Gardens and the City and specialise in a quality stock of London images, including gardens and heritage sites. With our constantly expanding library of photographs, we aim to represent and document what is essentially London life and landscape, both historically and into the future. Also available are many thousands of b/w images of the USA.
Quantity** Format S/M/L Colour D B/W

Colin Baxter Photography Ltd
Unit 2/3, Block 6, Caldwellside Industrial Estate, Lanark ML11 6SR
Tel: 0555 65022
Contact: Mike Rensner
Fax: 0555 4775

The distinctive atmospheric landscapes of Colin Baxter. Large collections on Scotland — our speciality — the Lake District, Yorkshire, the Cotswolds, France and Iceland. Also a special collection on the work of Scottish architect and designer, Charles Rennie Mackintosh.
Quantity** Format S Colour D

BBC Hulton Picture Library
See The Hulton Picture Company

BBC Photograph Library
Unit 1, 29 North Acton Road, Harlesden, London NW10 6PE
Tel: 081 743 8000 ext 2988
Contact: Margaret Kirby

The library is the BBC's unique archive collection of stills, dating back to 1922 and the earliest days of radio and television broadcasting equipment and premises. The library retains mainly BBC copyright material and consists of over 2 million colour and b/w images, constantly updated with new material from all parts of the BBC. Stills can be researched by name, programme title or subject. No origianl material is loaned. Copyright clearance is the responsibility of the user. Visitors welcome by appointment from 9.30 — 5.30, Monday — Friday.
Quantity**** Format S/M Colour A-B-C-D B/W

Beken of Cowes Ltd
16 Birmingham Road, Cowes, Isles of Wight PO31 7BH
Tel: 0983 297311
Contact: Kenneth J Beken
Fax: 0983 291059

Specialists in maritime subjects from 1888 to the present day. 100,000 medium format transparencies plus 75,000 b/w images. Subjects include worlwide ocean racing, Americas Cup, J-Class era, schooners, steam yachts, liners, power boats, cruising, Tall ships, etc. Worldwide commisions undertaken.
Quantity*** Format M/L Colour A-B-C-D B/W

Ivan J. Belcher Colour Picture Library
34 Berry Croft, Abingdon, Oxon OX14 1JL
Tel: 0235 521524
Contact: Ivan J Belcher

Extensive colour picture library specialising in top quality transparencies depicting the British scene in medium and large format, mainly of recent origin and constantly being updated. Thousands of images of cities, towns, picturesque harbours, rivers and canals, villages, cottages, rural scenes and traditions, photographed throughout the seasons. In-depth coverage of many locations and subjects including steam traction engines. Suitable for greeting cards, calendars, books, brochures and advertising.
Quantity ** Format M Colour D

BFI Stills, Posters and Designs
21 Stephen St., London W1 1PL
Tel: 071 255 1444
Contact: Bridget Kinally
Fax: 071 323 9260
Telex: 27624

About 3 million b/w original photographs, colour transparencies, posters, set and costume designs, illustrating the history of world cinematography c1895 to the present day. Films by titles/personality, film studios, cinema buildings, history of television. Special emphahsis throughout on British cinema and television. By appointment, Tuesday — Friday, 11.00-5.30. No loans. Duplicate b/w and colour transparencies available for a fee. Copyright clearance responsibility of the user. Printed catalogue available.
Quantity**** Format S/M/L Colour A-B-C-D B/W

John Birdsall Photography
74 Raleigh Street, Nottingham NG7 4DL
Tel: 0602 782645
Contact: Helen Bridges
Fax: 0602 785546

A multi-cultural, social-documentary library comprising a good collection of colour transparencies and prints and over 20,000 top quality b/w photographs. This collection, built up over twelve years, explores many contemporary social issues. Categories include children, housing, education, old age, youth, work and services and in addition, Nottingham and the surrounding areas, depicted in a wide range of colour and b/w images. A prompt and reliable picture service operates. Commissions undertaken.
Quantity** Format S Colour D B/W

Birmingham Public Libraries
Central Library, Paradise Circus, Birmingham B3 3HQ
Tel: 021 235 4549
Contact: Phillip Allen
Fax: 021 236 2112

Several important topographical collections. The principal ones being prints and negatives by Sir Benjamin Stone (1838-1914), Francis Bedford (1816-1894) and Francis Frith (1822-1898). The Stone Collection comprises 22,000 images (1880-1910) including customs, occupations, events, portraits and topographical views. The Bedford Collection is 3,000 images of SW England, W Midlands and Wales (1860-1890). The Frith Collection is 310,000 negatives from 1886-1965, indexed. The library also holds topographical prints of China, India, Sri Lanka and some European countries. Aslo 100,000 prints and negatives relating to Birmingham and its immediate environs and some railway material.
Quantity **** B/W

Anthony Blake
54 Hill Rise, Richmond, Surrey TW10 6UB
Tel: 081 940 7583/4
Contact: Julia Cooper
Fax: 081 948 1224

Specialist in food and wine. All colour coverage of cooking and finished dishes, restaurants and chefs, agriculture, vineyards and wine production, fishing and so on. Mainly 35mm but other formats are represented. Land and seascapes, skies and travel. Commissions undertaken. Catalogue available on request.
Quantity*** Format S/M/L Colour B-C-D

John Blake Picture Library
7 High Street, Thornbury, Bristol BS12 2AE
Tel: 0454 418321
Contact: John Blake
Fax: 0454 416636

The general topography of Britain, Europe and the rest of the world in all format transparencies and b/w. Constantly expanding stock includes landscapes, countryside, churches, architecture, cities, towns, villages, gardens, people at work and at play. Comprehensive collection on the Cotswolds and the Badminton and Gatcombe Horse Trials. Climbers and mountains of Himalayas, Antarctica, Alps, Africa, Norway and the Americas. Incorporated photographers available for commissions.
Quantity** Format S/M/L Colour C-D B/W

BMV Picturebank International Photo Library
79 Farringdon Road, London, EC1M 3JY
Tel: 071 405 5021
Contact: Nigel Messett
Fax: 071 831 2982

Expanding collection of very good quality colour transparencies in all formats. Main area of specialisation is world travel. Good selection also available on many other subjects especially landscapes, agriculture, architecture, birds, flowers, watersports, industry and technology and sunsets and sunrises. Commissions undertaken, home and abroad. Colour poster and full list of covered subjects available on request.
Quantity** Formats S/M/L Colour D

Janet & Colin Bord

See Fortean Picture Library

Boys Syndication

Red House, Newbourn, Woodbridge, Suffolk IP12 4PX
Tel: 0473 36333
Contact: Pamela Boys
Fax: 0394 380433

Specialised collection of Michael Boys international interiors, gardens, wine and food, lighting, girls and other creative images. Jacqui Hurst graden library containing features, plants, vegetables and wildflowers. Formats 35mm and larger, all edited for quality. Research to client's brief. Editorial ideas and whole books produced.
Quantity*** Format S/M Colour B-C-D

Bridgeman Art Library Ltd
19 Chepstow Road, London W2 5BP
Tel: 071 727 4065/229 7420
Contact: Harriet Bridgeman
Fax: 071 792 8509
Telex: 265208 ARTPIX

A colour library specialising in high quality, large format transparencies of paintings and works of art from antiquity to the present day, covering social and general history, battles, personalities and transportation, also furniture, glass, ceramics, silver, needlework, etc. Fully computerised. Agents for numerous publishers, museums and galleries including Art Resource and Superstock International New York, Photographie Giraudon, Paris and Index, Madrid.
Quantity** Format M/L Colour C-D Illustration

Britain on view Photographic Library
See Syndication International Ltd

Bubbles Photolibrary
23a Benwell Road London N7 7BL
Tel: 071 609 4547
Contact: Loisjoy Thurstun

A young, rapidly expanding specialist photo library dealing with babies, child development, pregnancy and women's health. Mostly colour on 35mm and medium format, although a number of b/w prints are held. Subjects not on file can be commissioned or covered by contributing photographers where sufficient notice is given.
Quantity** Format S/M Colour D B/W

Builder Group picture Library
Builder House, 1 Millharbour, London E14 9RA
Tel: 071 537 2222 ext 6243
Contact: Janique Helson
Fax: 071 537 2019

A comprehensive collection of colour and b/w photographs on 35mm and medium format, based on the fourteen magazines published by the Group, specifically; *Building, Chartered Surveyor Weekly,* and *Building Services.* The collection includes images on the various aspects of construction, housing, building and building services as well as the personalities of the industry. Also, up-to-date images of current construction sites in Britain, primarily London.
Quantity** Format S/M Colour D B/W

Buisness Magazine Picture Library
234 King's Road London SW3 5UA
Tel: 071 351 7351
Contact: Trudi Samuel
Fax: 071 351 2794
Telex: 914549 ITNMAG G

The definitive monthly, glossy, business magazine with a large amount of original material on file — which is constantly being added to. 35mm and medium format transparencies, b/w prints and illustrations available. Specialists in portraits of international business personalities and companies and wide coverage of city guides worldwide.
Quantity** Format S/M Colour D B/W Illustration

Calendar Concepts & Design
33 Albury Avenue Isleworth Middx TW7 5HY
Tel: 081 847 3777
Contact: Michael Brown
Fax: 081 568 2402
Telex: 924150 ADLIB G

This specialist agency provides a unique service to calendar publishers and last year was responsible for the content of more than fifty calendars. Representing leading photographers who are pre-eminent in their field, they can deliver complete calendar concepts for retail, bespoke or stock advertising clients. All tradtional calendar subjects are covered in depth — glamour — landscapes — transport — nature — sport. Innovative themes are being developed constantly to satisfy the increasing demand for new products. An illustrated book featuring the work of twelve photographers is available free of charge to calendar publishers. Please note this agency is unable to supply general stock requests.
Quantity** Format S/M/L Colour C-D

Camera Press Ltd
Russell Court, Coram Street, London WC1H 0NB
Tel: 071 837 4488/9393/1300/0606
Contact: Roger Wemyss-Brooks
Fax: 071 278 5126
Telex: 21654

Founded in 1947 by the late Tom Blau, this collection has a vast range of high quality photographs, both b/w and colour. Subject coverage is general with particular strengths in portraits and Royalty. New material is added daily from photographers and agencies around the world. Camera Press represents some of the best names in the business — Snowdon, Lichfield, Donovan, Beaton, Baron, Parkinson, Karsh of Ottawa, Dorothy Wilding, Prince Andrew... The collection currently numbers some 8 million images.
Quantity**** Format S/M/L Colour A-B-C-D B/W Illustration

'Camera Ways' Ltd
Court View, Egerton, Nr Ashford, Kent TN27 9BD
Tel: 023376 454/0860 506297
Contact: Derek Budd

An expanding collection of 35mm colour transparencies by television cameraman Derek Budd. Specialising in countryside and natural history programmes, his networked creative photography has won many international and Royal Television Society awards. Subjects include aerial locations, landscapes and people of southern England, Greece and the Falkland islands. A comprehensive collection of various habitats, wild flowers, butterflies, dragonflies, aquatic life, birds, fungi and insects. Character studies of country people, traditional crafts and village scenes. Occasional commissions possible.
Quantity* Format S Colour D

Camerapix
8 Ruston Mews, London W11 1RB
Tel: 071 221 0249
Contact: Debbie Granger
Fax: 071 792 8105

More than half a million 35mm medium format colour transparencies taken on assignments thoughout Africa, the Middle East and Asia during the last 25 years. African coverage provides portraits of political leaders and personalities, agriculture, industry, ethnic cultures and landscapes. Extensive portfolios on African wildlife, including rare and little known species. The Middle East and Asia includes heads of state, cities, industries, indigenous cultures and an outstanding Islamic portfolio showing every aspect of the Holy Cities of Mecca dn Medina and the rites of the annual pilgrimage (Haj). Requests not held in London may be accessed from our extensive collection in Nairobi.
Quantity** Format S/M Colour B-C-D

The Casement Collection
2 Frobisher Crescent, Stanwell, Staines TW19 7DX
Tel: 0784 254918
Contact: Jack Casement

Based on the personal collection of Jack Casement, but now being expanded with work by other photographers, the Casement Collection is an extensive international travel library of medium format colour transparencies and b/w prints of destinations from Abu Dhabi to Zimbabwe. Well noted for its creative element beyond the 'beach and palm tree' syndrome. The library contains only originals, no dupes, and is particularly strong on North America and the Gulf. General list available on request.
Quantity** Format M Colour D B/W

J Allan Cash Ltd
74 South Ealing Road, London W5 4QB
Tel: 081 840 4141
Contact: Alan Denny
Fax: 081 566 2568

From it origins, marketing J Allan Cash's extensive output, the library has undergone considerable change of direction over the past few years and now represents 300+photographers, who contribute on a regular basis, introducing new material into the files. We stock approximately 250,000 colour transparencies in all formats and a similar number of b/w prints, all edited to reproductionstandard, cross-indexed and filed for easy access. Coverage includes worldwide travel and documentary as well as large general sections on people, natural history, space, sport and activities and many other subjects.
Quantity**** Fromat S/M/L Colour B-C-D B/W

Celtic Picture Agency/Asiantaeth Llunlau Celtaldd
4 Rhodfa Gwilym, St Asaph, Clwyd, North Wales LL17 0UU
Tel: 074574 395
Contact: Mike Thomas

Established in 1985 and growing daily, with contributions from some fifteen Welsh photographers dotted around the principality and happy to accept commissions for material stock. The library is extremely strong on environmental material including current issues relating to conservation, second homes, farming, developmet in the countryside and National Parks, tourism expansion, employment creation in rural areas, etc. It holds a wealth of scenic material, many depicting historical sites both inland and on the coast. Requests by phone between 9am and 9pm. Urgent orders despatched Datapost or according to clients' wishes.
Quantity** Format S/M Colour D B/W

Cephas Picture Library
20 Trafalgar Drive, Walton-on-Thames, Surrey KT12 1NZ
Tel: 0932 241903
Contact: Mick Rock
Fax: 0932 241903

The most comprehensive collection available anywhere on the Wine Industry and vineyards of the world. Countries covered include France, Spain, Portugal, Italy, England, Switzerland, West Germany, USA, Canada, Australia, New Zealand, Japan and South Africa. Also the Scotch Whisky Industry. All on medium format. We are also a general library with good selections from the UK, Europe and the Far East. Orders despatched same day. Researchers welcome by appointment. We are only forty minutes from Central London. No service charge if material is used.
Quantity** Format S/M Colour D B/W

The Chatsworth Collection
Chatsworth House, Edensor, Bakewell, Derbyshire DE4 1PJ
Tel: 0246 582242
Contact: Christine Marshall
Fax: 0246 583464

This is a unique photo library of the treasures of Chatsworth, home of the Duke of Devonshire. From Elizabethan beginnings to Capability Brown's landscaping, the drawings of Rembrandt and Raphael to the paintings of Reynolds, Van Dyke, Poussin, Holbein, Rembrandt, Landseer and others, the Library of over 40,000 volumes to the countless other treasures of Chatsworth. One of the greatest collections in the world. Not only an academic fine art library but by using imagery from wall coverings, lacquerwork, inlays, porcelain and carvings, both interior and exterior, this is also a collection which can be used im many commercial applications.
Quantity* Format M/L Colour D Illustration

The Childrens' Photo Library
Alfa Studio, St. Thomas's Church Hall, East Row, London W10 5BX
Tel: 081 969 6827
Contact: Fiona Pragoff
Fax: 071 409 2869

An extensive personal collection of 35mm, medium format and b/w of children from birth onwards. The library consists of both studio and location work covering a wide range of subjects and activities. The collection has expanded and developed over the last ten years of work in advertising, editorial and publishing. Subjects not on file can be commissioned.
Quantity Format S/M Colour D B/W**

Christel Clear Marine Photography
Roselea, Church Lane, Awbridge, Nr Romsey, Hampshire SO51 0HN
Tel: 0794 41081
Contact: Nigel Dowden
Fax: 0794 40890

Formed in 1986, this specialist library has grown from the partnership of photographer Christel Dowden and husband Nigel, a working writer. Both are experienced yachtsmen. The emphasis of the library is on yacht racing from international Grand Prix events to local regattas. Originally news orientated, the library now holds several thousand colour and b/w images of water related activities worldwide. Subjects covered include racing yachts, cruising and classic yachts, cruising grounds, coastal and travel scenes. Both sail and power yachting are covered in 35mm and medium format. Suppliers of illustrated feature articles to non specialist sources. Commisssions undertaken worldwide.
Quantity Format S/M Colour D B/W**

Christian Aid Photo Library
PO Box 100, London SE1 7RT
Tel: 071 620 4444
Contact: Joseph Cabon
Fax: 071 620 0719

A specialist library of pictures from Africa, Asia and Latin America. Most are on development themes, agriculture, health, education, urban and rural life etc. All relate to small scale, community-based programmes set up by people working to claim or keep their rights or to improve their environment.
Quanity* Format S Colour D B/W**

Christie's Colour Library
8 King Street, St James's, London SW1Y 6QT
Tel: 071 839 9060 ext 2967
Contact: Claudia Brigg
Fax: 071 839 1611
Telex: 916429

A library of 60,000 high quality transparencies of all subjects illustrated in colour in Christie's Sales Catalogues from Leonardo to Beuys and Japanese swords to Bugatti furniture. The main emphasis is on Art Nouveau and Art Deco, Japanese and Chinese Art, furniture, ceramics, jewellery, silver, sculpture and, of course, painting. Also cars, boys, musical instruments, books and manuscripts, clocks, antiquities, collectibles and others. More than 10,000 new images every year.
Quantity* Format M/L Colour B-C-D B/W Illustration**

Phillip Craven Worldwide Photo-Library
Surrey Studios, 21 Nork Way, Nork, Banstead, Surrey SM7 1PB
Tel: 0737 373737
Contact: Philip Craven

Colour transparencies in medium and large format including worldwide travel, wildlife and pictorial. Specialist coverage of British scenes, cities, towns, villages, countryside, gardens, historic buildings, castles, cottages, London, landscapes and wildlife. Commissions personally undertaken.
Quantity Format M/L Colour C-D**

Lupe Cunha/Children Photography
Second Floor, 843-845 Green Lanes, London N21 2RX
Tel: 081 360 0144
Contact: Lupe Cunha
Fax: 081 886 6812

Children Photography. Over 10,000 images on all aspects - from pregnancy and babies to school - inclusive. Suitable for advertising, publishing, editorial and greeting card markets. Growing section on health and womens' interests and occupations. Twice annual programme of photographic shoots on specific subject areas. Contact us for current schedule. Brazil Photo-Agency is a general collection of 3,000 images on Brazilian life, tourism, nature and scenics, representing the work of 15 Brazilian photographers, including Lupe Cunha's work. Regular visits to Brazil ensure new material. Commissions undertaken at competitive prices for material of interest to the library. Portfolio and brochure available.
Quantity ** Format S/M Colour D B/W

Sue Cunningham Photographic
56 Chatham Road, Kingston-upon-Thames, Surrey KT1 3AA
Tel: 081 541 3024
Contact: Sue Cunningham

Around 20,000 top-quality images of Brazil make this the first library to call for your advertising and editorial needs. Mainly colour, with a wide range of subjects from industry to Indians, Ronnie Biggs to rainforests, stock is updated by regular visits to Brazil. Clients receive a personal service and commissions can be included in forthcoming trips. Inquiries about features are welcomed; we write too! Telephone for our free listing, covering 35,000 images - not only of Brazil.
Quantity ** Format S/M Colour D B/W

James Davis Travel Photography
30 Hengistbury Road, New Milton, Hampshire BH25 7LU
Tel: 0425 610328
Contact: James Davis
Fax: 0425 638402

James Davis' library has been built up over 20 years of his own travels and, in recent years, with the work of photographers in the UK and overseas. People, places, emotive scenes and tourism are the specialisation of this library. Apart from continuing to travel worldwide for new stock photography, he will always consider combining assignments - if travel is provided and the library retains a selection of the photographs obtained. In this way, considerable savings may be made over the cost of a normal commission or even libary fees. Selections normally sent same day by post or Red Star.
Quantity * Format S/M Colour B-C-D B/W**

Peter Dazeley Photography
The Studios, 5 Heathman's Road, Parsons Green, London SW6 4TJ
Tel: 071 736 3171
Contact: Peter Dazeley
Fax: 071 736 3356

Peter Dazeley, a top name in golf photography, has a large library in Fulham, London, covering the last two decades of the sport. His material is shot at most of the major tournaments and consists of colour transparencies and b/w photographs of players, both male and female, golf courses and related miscellaneous material.
Quantity** Format S/M Colour B-C-D B/W**

Douglas Dickins Photo Library
2 Wessex Gardens, Golders Green, London NW11 9RT
Tel: 081 455 6221
Contact: Douglas Dickins

Worldwide library in colour, 35mm and medium format and b/w, specialising in educational work in Asia and especially India. Strong on Indonesia, Japan, USA and Canada. Also covered, Hong Kong, Burma, Cambodia (Angkor Wat), Sri Lanka, China, Pakistan (Karakorms), Iran, Egypt, Singapore, Thailand, South Korea, Taiwan, Tunisia, Morocco, Uganda, Kenya, Sierra Leone, South Africa, Australia, New Zealand, Fiji, Equador, Peru (Machhupicchu). Britain, with emphasis on historical sites and houses, scenics, people, religions, customs, archaeology, folklore and historic buildings.
Quantity* Format S/M Colour B-C-D B/W**

C M Dixon
The Orchard, Marley Lane, Kingston, Canterbury, Kent CT4 6JH
Tel: 0227 830075
Contact: Michael Dixon
Fax: 0227 830075

Colour transparencies in 35mm and medium format, specialising in ancient civilisations, archaeology and art, especially Stone, Bronze and Iron Ages, Greek, Roman, Scythian, Celtic, Byzantine, Viking, Egyptian and Mesopotamian. Ethnology, mythology, world religion, museum objects. Agriculture, architecture, geography, geology, meteorology, mountains, occupations, scenic, travel, people and places in most of Europe including USSR, Egypt, Ethiopia, Iceland, Morocco, Sri Lanka, Tunisia and Turkey.
Quantity*** Format S/M Colour A-B-C-D B/W

Dominic Photography
9a Netherton Grove, London SW10 9TQ
Tel: 071 352 6118
Contact: Zoë Dominic
Fax: 071 351 0058

Dance, opera, theatre, ballet, films and television - an extensive coverage in colour, 35mm and medium format and b/w of all aspects of the entertainment world. The library consists of over 250,000 transparencies and negatives shot from 1957 to the present day of live performance, back-stage, studio shots and portraits of dancers, singers, actors and musicians. Whilst mostly shot in the UK, the library includes material photographed in Europe, America and Japan.
Quantity**** Format S/M Colour A-B-C-D B/W

E T Archive
19 Albany Street, London NW1 4DX
Tel: 071 584 3137
Contact: Anne-Marie Ehrlich
Fax: 071 823 8996

History in Art. Large format colour transparencies and b/w prints. Paintings, engravings and sculpture and some contemporary photographs. Subjects range from archaeology, botany, fashion, manuscripts, portraits and topography to zoology. Special collection on ancient civilisations, Australiana, music and militaria. We handle the Elek archive, The Garrick Club, Kea's garden pictures and Staffordshire Polytechnic's ceramic collection as well as material from English and continental photographers. An up-to-date catalogue is always available as well as expert picture research.
Quantity** Format L Colour C-D B/W Illustration

Patrick Eagar photography
5 Ennerdale Road, Kew Gardens, Surrey TW9 3PG
Tel: 081 940 9269
Contact: Patrick Eagar
Fax: 081 332 1229

The Cricket Library comprises colour and b/w 35mm photographs dating from 1965, including detailed coverage of every Test match played in England since 1972. Overseas tours are covered in some detail. The material includes cricket grounds, player portraits, action shots and historic moments from the village green to the great Test arenas worldwide. It is well indexed.
The Wine Library is in colour and concentrates on carefully captioned photographs of the vineyards, grapes, cellars and winemakers of France, Australia, New Zealand, Italy, Spain, Portugal, England and Greece.
Quantity**** Format S Colour B-C-D B/W

Edifice
14 Doughty Street, London WC1N 2PL
Tel: 071 405 9395
Contact: Philippa Lewis
Fax: 071 267 3632

Buildings of all kinds and their immediate surroundings. Types range from almshouses to watermills by way of bungalows and railway stations; materials from corrugated iron to marble. All varieties of architectural triumphs and horrors, conversions, dereliction, urban and rural features and gardens. Pictures are categorised by styles, periods, building materials and architects. We specialise in details and ornament, particularly vernacular - doors, windows, ironwork, fences, etc - and in providing accurate and detailed captions. Good coverage of American domestic architecture, French and Italian as well as of British. Visits welcome by appointment.
Quantity** Format S Colour C-D

EMAP Classic Archives
EMAP National Publications Ltd, Bushfield House, Orton Centre, Peterborough PE2 0UW
Tel: 0733 237111
Contact: Brian Wolley
Fax: 0733 231137

A rare and comprehensive archive covering the history of motor cycles and motorcycling and based on material from The Motor Cycle and Motor Cycling, published between 1903 and 1980. Text can be recovered and photographs copied. PMT's of technical drawings can be provided. No original material leaves the premises. Four days' notice is required for copies of historic photographs.
Quantity**** B/W Illustration

Empics Ltd
26 Musters Road, West Bridgford,
Nottinghamshire NG2 7PL
Tel: 0602 455885
Contact: Mervyn Pamment
Fax: 0602 455243

A relatively new library, established in 1985, of over 30,000 pictures in colour and b/w covering international and national sport, news and features. Colour material is available in both transparency and print formats. In addition, b/w and stock colour can be transmitted from our modern electronic picture desk within minutes of a request from clients with a wire receiver. Staff photographers can undertake commissions worldwide.
Quantity** Format S Colour D B/W

English Heritage Picture Library
Room 517, Fortress House, 23 Savile Row,
London W1X 1AB
Tel: 071 973 3338/9
Contact: Lucy Bunning
Fax: 071 973 3001

A unique historical archive and expanding contemporary collection containing thousands of original large format transparencies plus b/w negatives of all English Heritage properties in care. Castles, abbeys, standing stones, mills, Roman ruins, ancient monuments, paintings, churches and gardens. Also special events such as English Civil War and medieval tournament re-enactments on 35mm.
Quantity*** Format S/M/L Colour B-C-D B/W Illustration

Robert Estall Photographs
Falcon House, 12/14 Swan Street, Boxford, Colchester,
Essex CO6 5NZ
Tel: 0787 210111
Contact: Robert Estall
Fax: 0787 211440

This rapidly expanding collection of 35mm and medium format
transparencies is almost entirely the work of Robert Estall and consists
of diverse documentary and evocative photographs from Britain,
Europe and North America. As well as a good general range of
subjects, there are special collections on standing stones and
megalithic sites, cheese and cheese-making, transport, domestic and
farm animals and sites involving hauntings and legends. Also African
adornments and portraits by Angela Fisher.
Quantity* Format S/M Colour B-C-D**

Greg Evans International (Photo Library)
91 Charlotte Street, London W1P 1LB
Tel: 071 636 8238 (3 lines)
Contact: Susie
Fax: 071 637 1439

Comprehensive general colour library with over 200,000
transparencies in all formats and constant updating of material.
Featuring Greg Evan's own worldwide travel and skiing collection
and general subjects from 300 photographers. Subjects covered
include abstracts, aircraft, art, animals, antiques, beaches, business,
children, computers, couples, families, food and restaurants, glamour,
industry, nature history, skies, sunsets, soft focus, sports (action and
leisure), UK scenics and worldwide travel. Visitors welcome.
Combined commissions undertaken. Photographers' submissions
welcome.
Quantity* Format S/M/L Colour D**

Mary Evans Picture Library
59 Tranquil Vale, Blackheath, London SE3 0BS
Tel: 081 318 0034
Contact: Mary Evans
Fax: 081 852 7211

General historic collection, all subjects and periods to circa 1939,
mostly prints and ephemera but some photographs and several
thousand medium format colour transparencies. Emphasis on social
conditions, history of technology and visual documentation of the
past. Specialist material on the paranormal, from levitation to UFO's.
Long runs of illustrated periodicals, British and foreign. Special
collections: Sigmund Freud photographs, Society for Psychical
Research, London University Harry Price Collection, The Fawcett
Library (women's rights), Bruce Castle Museum (daily life 1850-1950),
Ernst Dryden Collection (fashion/publicity early 20th Century).
Quantity** Format M B/W Illustration**

EWA Photo Library
21 Albert Street, London NW1 7LU
Tel: 071 388 2828
Contact: Liz Whiting
Fax: 071 387 1615

Specialist library of colour transparencies covering all aspects of
contemporary interior decoration, gardening and architecture. A
group of 30 photographers, based at home and abroad ensure new
material is added on a regular basis. The library of individual images
is classified by room, type of garden and cross-referenced by suject.
Clients are welcome to search for themselves or we offer an intelligent
and fast research service. There is always a selection of new features
showing different types of homes and gardens - London family house,
NY loft, Dockland conversion, Scandinavian garden, Californian
beach house etc. An A-Z of garden plants has been commenced
recently.
Quantity* Format S/M/L Colour C-D**

The Express Picture Library
Ludgate House, 245 Blackfriars Road, London SE1 9UX
Tel: 071 922 7902-3-4-5
Contact: Dennis Hart
Fax: 071 922 7966
Telex: 21841

A general agency handling pictures, text illustrations and cartoons
from Express Newspapers (Daily Express, Sunday Express, Sunday
Express Magazine, Daily Star). The library holds colour in most
formats and b/w on a range of sujects including Royalty, fashion,
events, personalities, nostalgia, sport, cars, showbiz, etc. Pictures by
staff photographers and handled on behalf of certain freelance
photographers.
Quantity** Format S/M Colour D B/W Illustration**

Eye Ubiquitous
1 Brunswick Road, Hove, East Sussex BN3 1DG
Tel: 0273 26135
Contact: Paul Seheult
Fax: 0273 820775

The collection is continually growing and now holds images from 60
photographers worldwide. Subject matter varies from UK landscapes
through the opening of the Berlin Wall to a large collection on Japan.
There is a strong emphasis on adults and children in all aspects of
their lives. Where possible, pictures not on file will be shot in the studio
or on location.
Quantity Format S/M Colour D**

Chris Fairclough Colour Library
Studio 65, Smithbrook Kilns, Cranleigh, Surrey GU6 8JJ
Tel: 0483 277992
Contact: Bridget Sherlock

The library handles the work of some 200 photographers, some from
overseas and consists of over 80,000 colour transparencies from 90
countries - mostly 35mm and medium format. Subjects are varied and
diverse, covering agriculture, education, industry, religion, sport,
transport and wildlife (a particularly good coverage of British wild
flowers). Our 'keyword' searching system can usually answer
enquiries within minutes and despatch material the same day. Lists of
subjects available. We have full studio facilities on site and can
arrange a shoot of a particular shot not already covered, at the same
cost as if supplied from stock. Researchers are welcome by
appointment between 9.30 and 4.00 daily. The coffee is free.
Quantity* Format S/M Colour D**

Falklands Pictorial

see **David Muscroft Picture Library**

Farmers Publishing Group Picture Library
69-73 Manor Road, Greenfield House, Wallington, Surrey SM6 0DE
Tel: 081 661 4914
Contact: Peggy Wilson

Probably Europe's biggest agriculture picture library with more than a
million photographs available for loan. Every aspect of farming and
country life in colour and b/w. Free colour brochure available on
request.
Quantity** Format S/M Colour A-B-C-D B/W**

Feature-Pix Colour Library/World Pictures
1st Floor, 85a Great Portland Street, London W1N 5RA
Tel: 071 437 2121/436 0440
Contact: Gerry Brenes
Fax: 071 439 1307

Specialised collection aimed at the travel and holiday market. Over 300,000 transparencies in medium format, showing countries, cities and resorts throughout the world, likely to interest tour operators and others producing brochures. Files also include a wide selection of 'emotive' holiday material suitable for cover and display use. Coverage of popular resort areas updated annually. Photographers available for assignment.
Quantity**** Format M/L Colour D

Paul Felix
Hornbeam House, Robinson Lane, Woodmancote, Nr Cirencester
GL7 7EW
Tel: 0285 83703
Contact: Diana Alexander

A collection of colour transparencies of all aspects of modern country life, this small library specialises in high quality work on craftsman tradition and modern crafts from charcoal burning and stonewalling to baskets for hot-air balloons and acrylic jewellery, with portraits and activities of the men and women who work around the country. Most are available with full text. Also a large collection of landscapes of the Cotswolds and the Thames Valley, which have appeared in the book A Year on the Thames, a full colour portrait of the river throughout the seasons.
Quantity** Format S/M/L Colour D

ffotograff
10 Kyveilog Street, Pontcanna, Cardiff CF1 9JA
Tel: 0222 236879
Contact: Patricia Aithie

Expanding library and photo agency. Quality international colour material including Middle and Far East, China, Australia - and Wales. Reportage for editorial and commercial use, foreign cultures, people, architecture and the natural environment. Accompanying text if required. Commissions for photo-features UK and abroad undertaken by freelance photographers Patricia and Charles Aithie.
Quantity** Format S/M/L Colour D B/W

Financial Times Picture Library
The Financial Times, No 1 Southwark Bridge, London SE1 9HL
Tel: 071 873 3484
Fax: 071 407 5700

The Financial Times Picture Collection consists of around 500,000 items and is extremely diverse in its subject matter. The great strength of the collection rests on the comprehensive personality files built up over the last ten years, covering key statesmen, politicians and financial figures worldwide. Our photographers tour the world covering the major financial centres and have built up a fascinating selection of pictures covering industry, banking and agriculture, in both the industrialised countries and the Third World.
Quantity** Format S Colour D B/W

Fine Art Photographic Library
2a Milner Street, London SW3 2PU
Tel: 071 589 3127/584 1944
Contact: Linda Hammerbeck

Around 20,000 large format transparencies of mainly 19th and early 20th Century paintings. Categories include genre, marine, landscape, seasonal, floral, religious and historical. Suitable for use in advertising, television, print, stationery and book publishing. Highly commercial, they are available also for the packaging of contemporary toiletries and cassettes, etc. Clients by appointment. Research carried out for a fee. Colour brochure available on request.
Quantity** Format L Colour D Illustration

Werner Forman Archive Ltd
36 Camden Square, London NW1 9XA
Tel: 071 267 1034
Contact: Barbara Heller
Fax: 071 267 6026

Medium format colour and b/w photographs specialising in the art and cultures of ancient civilisations, the Near and Far East and primitive societies of the world. Many subjects are comprehensively covered particularly Vikings, ancient Mexico, North American Indian archaelogy, ancient Japan, Africa, ancient Egypt, Assyria and China. The archive contains a number of rare collections including oriental and primitive jewellery, sex and fertility magic and the white man as depicted in the art of Africa, Asia and the Americas. Tantric, Dogon and Vietnamese art, masks, tapestries, silks and embroideries, etc. Photographs cross-reference and subject lists available.
Quantity** Format M

Format Partners Photo Library
19 Arlington Way, London EC1R 1UY
Tel: 071 883 0292
Contact: Maggie Murray

Format represents the work of 18 women photographers. An expanding range of subjects in colour and b/w reflects the social, economic and political life of people in Britain and abroad. We specialise in women's issues, work, health, education, the elderly and the very young. Good coverage of Black and Asian cultures, people with disabilities, the environment, politics, gay issues, trade union issues, demonstrations, Northern Ireland, transport and leisure activities. Countries include Africa, Asia, the Americas, Caribbean, Europe, Middle East, Soviet Union, China and SE Asia. We offer a friendly, efficient service and researchers are welcome by appointment. Photographers available for commission.
Quantity** Format S Colour C-D B/W

Fortean Picture Library
Melysfan, Llangwm, Corwen, Clwyd LL21 0RD
Tel: 049 082 472
Contact: Janet Bord
Fax: 049 082 321

A pictorial archive of mysteries and strange phenomena worldwide including clairvoyance, cryptozoology, dowsing, dragons, ectoplasm, fairies, ghosts, giants, haunted sites, lake monsters, levitation, leys, manlike monsters (like Bigfoot), mediums, metal bending, poltergeists, PSI, sea monsters, shamanism, stigmata, UFO's, visions, werewolves, witchcraft and much more. The archive is managed by Janet and Colin Bord, authors of books on mysteries, whose photographs of prehistoric sities, antiquities, churches, countryside and folklore of Britain and Ireland are also available from the same address. 'Wales Scene' is a growing collection of Welsh pictures - landscape, towns and villages, churches, rural life and nature.
Quantity** Format S/M Colour C-D B/W

The Francis Frith Collection plc
Charlton Road, Andover, Hampshire SP10 3LE
Tel: 0264 53113/4
Contact: Ann Hutchings
Fax: 0264 332811

This collection contains over 330,000 photographs depicting some 4,000 towns and villages throughout the British Isles in the period 1860-1970, on average, 40 views for small towns and over 100 for large towns and cities. The collection is topographical and catalogued alphabetically by town. In many cases, photographs are available for the same location taken at regular intervals throughout the period. Several thousand are catalogued by theme, including canals, Royalty, blacksmiths, boats and ships, brewing and breweries, buses, butchers, camping, castles, etc. A list is available and the whole collection is being copied onto microfiche for the convenience of researchers.
Quantity**** B/W

The Garden Picture Library
Unit 15, Ransome's Dock, 35 Parkgate Road, London SW11 4NP
Tel: 071 228 4332
Contact: Sally Wood
Fax: 071 924 3267
Telex: 915270 SBOS G DP

Comprehensive archives of original colour transparencies in 35mm and medium format, covering all facets of gardens, portraits of plants, garden design and garden living. Continual supply of original features on historical and contemporary gardens from Europe, the Americas and Australia. A worldwide network of photographers is available to originate material to specific needs. Archive list is available on request.
Quantity* Format S/M Colour D**

Leslie Garland Picture Library
69 Fern Ave, Jesmond, Newcastle upon Tyne,
Tyne and Wear NE2 2QU
Tel: 091 281 3442
Contact: Leslie Garland

NE England is our speciality - architecture, backpacking, bridges, construction, countryside, civil engineering, ecology, environment, geography and geology, heritage, industry, leisure, mountains, natural history, scenics, seas and skies, towns and villages, transport, travel, wild flowers, etc. Other areas covered include the Lake District and Scotland, Europe and the Far East. Pictures are available in colour and b/w, 35mm and medium format, suitable for advertising, books, brochures, exhibitions, magazines, etc. Qualified photographers available to undertake commissions.
Quantity Format S/M Colour C-D B/W**

Genesis Space Photo Library
Peppercombe Lodge, Horns Cross, Bideford, Devon EX39 5DH
Tel: 0237 451756
Contact: Tim Furniss
Fax: 0237 451600
Telex: 9312131285 TF G

Specialist service from Tim Furniss, spaceflight journalist and author, with 25 years experience in the spaceflight writing industry. Genesis holds a comprehensive library of historical and contemporary spaceflight photographs, backed up by an expert knowledge of the industry, to provide the right photographs to meet the tightest brief. Colour transparencies, colour and b/w prints. Rockets - spacecraft - spacemen - Earth - Moon and planets. Research and reproduction fees negotiable.
Quantity* Format S/M Colour A-B-C-D B/W

GeoScience Features
6 Orchard Drive, Wye, Near Ashford, Kent TN25 5AU
Tel: 0233 812707
Contact: Dr Basil Booth
Fax: 0233 812707

Comprehensive and computerised library containing the world's principal source of volcanic phenomena. Extensive collections of rocks, minerals, fossils, animals, birds, botany, chemistry, Earth science, ecology, environment, geology, geography, habitats, landscapes, macro-biology, peoples, sky, weather, wildlife and zoology. Over 120,000 original colour transparencies in 35mm and medium format for advertising, calendars and books. Providing scientific detail with technical quality. Subject lists available on application.
Quantity* Format S/M Colour B-C-D Illustration**

Glamour International
Vision House, 16 Broadfield Road, Heeley, Sheffield S8 0XJ
Tel: 0742 589299
Contact: David Muscroft
Fax: 0742 550113

A major and rapidly expanding collection of glamour images of the highest quality. Medium format transparencies of the most beautiful models, ranging from 'page 3' studio shots to girls on beaches, at stately homes and many other locations. Pictures syndicated directly to many editorial users worldwide and to the UK calendar market. Our files also include beauty shots, keep-fit themes, make-up and romantic boy-girl themes. Specific commissions can be accommodated either in our studio or on frequent location shoots. Pictures dispatched same day.
Quantity Format M Colour D**

Martin & Dorothy Grace
40 Clipstone Avenue, Mapperley, Notts NG3 5JZ
Tel: 0602 208248
Contact: Dorothy Grace
Fax: 0602 626802

A rapidly expanding personal collection of 35mm transparencies portraying Britain's natural history. Specialities are native trees, shrubs and wild flowers and of these, we have a particularly comprehensive collection covering a significant proportion of the list and including many rare species. Also, an extensive range of habitats, landscapes and illustrations of ecological principles and conservation. Other subjects include birds and butterflies and a small, unusually diverse collection of other fauna. Photographs taken in a wide variety of locations with emphasis on a natural yet striking presentaton. Subject lists available on request.
Quantity Format S Colour D**

Sally and Richard Greenhill
357a Liverpool Road, London N1 1NL
Tel: 071 607 8549
Contact: Sally Neal

Continually expanding coverage of a social documentary nature. Our well established library covers, both at home and broad, such subjects as education, leisure, medicine, pregnancy and birth, child development and family life, poverty, urban environment, teenagers, old people, religion, transport, farming, industry, agriculture, etc. Also, a special sub-section on London's statues. Abroad, our already comprehensive coverage of modern China from 1971 has been enlarged by the inclusion of the SACU photo library. Good coverage of Hong Kong and the USA. Some material from Germany (handcrafts), Greece, Albania, Sri Lanka, Singapore, Borneo (long house life) and the Philippines.
Quantity** Format S Colour C-D B/W**

Greenpeace Communications Ltd
124 Cannon Workshops, West India Docks, London E14 9SA
Tel: 071 515 0275
Contact: Liz Somerville
Fax: 071 538 1177
Telex: 8953660

Colour and b/w photographs covering environmental issues and Greenpeace actions and campaigns. Subjects include industrial and nuclear waste dumping, the waste trade, acid rain, polluted rivers and seas, oil pollution, sewage dumping, CFC production, nuclear power/reprocessing/transport, nuclear testing and weapons, seals, whales, dolphins, turtles, kangaroos, destructive fishing techniques, deforestation, pesticides, rainforests, Pacific, Mediterranean, Antarctica, Eastern Europe.
Quantity Format S Colour C-D B/W**

Susan Griggs Agency Ltd

Unit 2B, 101 Farm Lane Trading Estate, London SW6 1QJ
Tel: 071 385 8112
Contact: Sandra Schadeberg
Fax: 071 381 0935
Telex: 265871 ref WQQ122

350,000 original colour transparencies, mostly 35mm, covering scenics and people worldwide, plus extensive files ranging through animals and birds, antiquities, babies and children, families, crafts, industry, plants, gardens and trees, sunsets, seascapes, transport, weather, wine and vineyards, etc. The library has recently moved into larger premises and intends to expand its choice in all areas. All library contributors are professional photographers. Clients by appointment or in-house research by an experienced team. Subject lists available on request. Photographic assignments undertaken by freelance photographers with worldwide editorial, corporate and advertising experience.

Quantity**** Format S Colour C-D

V K Guy Ltd

Silver Birches, Troutbeck, Windermere, Cumbria LA23 1PN
Tel: 05394 33519
Contact: Vic Guy
Fax: 05394 32971

20,000 (and increasing), medium and large format transparencies of British landscapes. Available for calendars, advertising, jigsaws, brochures, greeting cards, books, etc. We invite you to view this collection featuring the beautiful countryside and architectural heritage of Britain. The countryside is pictured throughout the year to catch the changing qualities and moods of the different seasons and includes dramatic atmospheric shots. Attractive studies of famous cities, towns and villages, traditional cottages, colourful gardens, scenic harbours and splendid castles and cathedrals. Colour brochure sent on request.

Quantity** Format M/L Colour D

Sonia Halliday Photographs

Primrose Cottage, Weston Turville, Bucks HP22 5SL
Tel: 029 661 2266
Contact: Sonia Halliday

Over 100,000 original transparencies. Specialists in stained glass, Biblical subjects in all media and Middle Eastern archaeological sites. Coverage in Egypt, Cyprus, Greece, Israel, Jordan, Turkey in archaeology, ethnology, geography, industry, and illuminated manuscripts. Christian/Islamic manuscripts from Bibliothèque Nationale. Hand painted 1840 engravings, Tassili cave paintings, Bushmen and African wildlife, Chartres Cathedral, Angers tapestries, Byzantine/Roman mosaics, murals, mythology, cloudscapes, landscapes, seascapes, Afghanistan, China, Crete, France, Britain, India, Italy, Nepal, Persia, Sicily, Spain, Tunisia, Yugoslavia. Aerial coverage of Israel, Jordan, Kibris (Northern Cyprus). Book jackets a speciality.

Quantity*** Format S/M Colour C-D B/W Illustration

Tom Hanley

61 Stephendale Road, Fulham, London SW6 2LT
Tel: 071 731 3525
Contact: Tom Hanley

Colour in 35mm and medium format and b/w covering people and places in London and many parts of England, Europe, Canada, India, the Phillipines, Brazil, China, Japan, Korea, Taiwan, Seychelles, Cayman Islands and the USA. Also some sixties material including The Beatles and other pop artists, the sailing of the Atlantic by Ridgeway and Blyth, the removal of London Bridge to America and the destruction of cattle through foot and mouth disease. Also First World War trenches at Vimy Ridge.

Quantity** Format S/M Colour B-C-D B/W

Robert Harding Picture Library Ltd

1st Floor, 58/59 Great Marlborough Street, London W1V 1DD
Tel: 071 287 5414
Contact: Jenny Pate
Fax: 071 631 1070

Our files now exceed 1 million colour transparencies and we welcome researchers to browse. Ask for our free colour catalogue with examples of the following subjects:
abstracts, activities, agriculture, animals, anthropology, archaeology, architecture, art, beauty, children, cities, commodities, computer graphics, crafts, customs, education, farming, fashion, food and drink, geography, girls, hobbies, industry, interiors, landscapes, medicine, natural history, people, space, sport, technology, transport, travel, etc. We represent the Rainbird Picture Library which includes extensive fine art and Tutankhamun, Alistair Cowen's Beauty Book, Victor Kennett Collection, Equinox Picture Library, The Chinese Exhibition and Financial Times Colour.

Quantity**** Format S/M/L Colour B-C-D B/W

Harpur Garden Library

44 Roxwell Road, Chelmsford, Essex CM1 2NB
Tel: 0245 257527
Contact: Jerry Harpur

Jerry Harpur is the photographer of Private Gardens of Australia and Creating Period Gardens. He has been photographing gardens, town and country, in Britain, Europe, Australia and North America for nearly ten years for book and magazine publishers and the library holds over 30,000 transparencies, mostly 35mm. A similar number of his pictures from other, different gardens, is held by EWA (071 388 3171) qv

Quantity** Format S/M Colour D

Hobbs Golf Collection

The Beeches, 18 East Corner, Worcester WR2 6BE
Tel: 0905 422162
Contact: Michael Hobbs

With twenty golf books published and many articles, Michael Hobbs knows the needs of writers, picture researchers and editors. A historian of the game from its beginnings at least seven centuries ago to the present day, he has unique insight into what pictures may be of use. Subjects include well known golfers since the 1840's, other golfing characters since 1502, paintings, other art forms and memorabilia from 1350, golf action from 1746, the written and printed word from 1457, early advertising from 1880 to 1930 and playing equipment from 1600. Golf course photography a speciality. Commissions accepted for tournaments and instruction.

Quantity** Format S Colour A-D B/W Illustration

Michael Holford Photo Library

119 Queens Road, Loughton, Essex IG10 1RR
Tel: 081 508 4358
Contact: Michael Holford
Fax: 081 508 3359

Art history in colour on medium and large format. Architecture and objects from pre-history to the 19th Century. Prehistoric, Sumerian, Babylonian, Hittite, Assyrian, Egyptian, Greek, Roman, Coptic, Islamic, European, Chinese, Japanese, Indian, Mayan, Aztec, Inca, African, Melanesian, Polynesian. Tombs, temples, churches, cathedrals, castles, houses, sculptures, ceramics, coins, maps, manuscripts, paintings, prints, terracottas, mosaics, textiles, Greek vases, stained glass, the Bayeaux Tapestry (complete in 80 sections), ivories, enamels, jewellery, frescoes, altarpieces, bronzes, Mughal miniatures, Hindu miniatures, Persian miniatures, ikons, early scientific instruments, early navigational instruments, early toys.

Quantity*** Format M/L Colour C-D

Holt Studios Ltd
The Courtyard, 24 High Street, Hungerford, Berks RG17 0NF
Tel: 0488 683523
Contact: Nigel Cattlin
Fax: 0488 683511
Telex: 848507 Ref. Holt

Pictorial and technical photographs on 35mm and medium format of world agriculture and horticulture. All factors associated with crop production and crop protection including healthy crops, weeds, pests, diseases, deficiencies, people and machines, livestock, husbandry and management, factors affecting the environment. Worldwide assignments undertaken.
Quantity** Format S/M Colour D

Houses and Interiors Photographic Features Agency
The Rockery, The Moor, Hawkhurst, Kent TN18 4NE
Tel: 0580 754078
Contact: Richard Wiles
Fax: 0580 754197

Rapidly expanding stock collection of top quality 35mm and medium format transparencies of stylish house interiors and exteriors, interior design, crafts, home renovation, practical step-by-step sequences, architectural details, regional building styles, gardens and general home interest topics. B/W also available. Dossiers on complete houses of all ages and styles plus their owners, including text. Commissions undertaken. Visiting researchers welcome; photographers submissions always sought. The agency are also experienced desktop pubishing packagers producing partworks, magazines and books: full writing, design, photographic, typesetting and editing facilities provided.
Quantity** Format S/M/L Colour D B/W

The Hulton Picture Company
Unique House, 21-31 Woodfield Road, London W9 2BA
Tel: 071 266 2662 (Pictures)
Contact: Milica Timotic
Fax: 071 289 6392
Tel: 071 266 2660 (Head Office)

This enormous resource comprises not only the Hulton Picture Collection based on the Picture Post Library together with over forty other individual collections but now includes the Keystone Collection of Keystone, Fox, Central Press and Three Lions. Coverage is comprehensive from pre-history to the 1980's with particular emphasis on social history, Royalty, sport, war and transport. The company is sole agent in the UK for the Bettmann Archive - New York.
Quantity**** Format S/M Colour A-B-C-D B/W

The Hutchison Library
118b Holland Park Avenue, London W11 4UA
Tel: 071 229 2743/727 6410
Contact: Michael Lee
Fax: 071 792 9259

Over half a million worldwide photographs in 35mm colour and b/w covering agriculture, art, crafts, ethnic, industry, landscape, medicine, religion, customs, urban and country life, war, disasters, transport. Also, the following collections: Disappearing World (ethnic minorities), Puttkamer (Amazon Indians), Long Search (world religions), Moser/Taylor (South American Indians), Felix Greene (China, North Vietnam, Tibet), Tribal Eye (tribal), Shogun Experience (Japan), Spirit of Asia, New Pacific and Durrell-McKenna, Kitzinger and Stoppard Collections on pregnancy, birth and human relations. Also David Hodge/Academia Medica Collection.
Quantity**** Format S/M Colour C-D B/W

ICCE Photo Library
Greenfield House, Guiting Power, Cheltenham, Glos GL54 5TZ
Tel: 0451 850 777
Contact: Kathleen Collier
Fax: 0451 850 705

A rapidly expanding collection of colour transparencies and b/w prints, specialising in conservation and environmental issues. Scenics and wildlife from Britain, Africa, South East Asia, the Middle East and more. Forests, mountains, grasslands, deserts, seas and rivers, animals in their natural habitats including excellent coverage of African mammals and birds. National parks and protected areas, forestry, agriculture and domestic livestock. People, cities, towns and villages, rich and poor. Environmental impact including pollution, poaching and trade in wildlife. All photo library income supports the work of the Centre in promoting conservation education in developing countries.
Quantity** Format S Colour D B/W

The Illustrated London News Picture Library
20 Upper Ground, London SE1 9FP
Tel: 071 928 6969
Contact: Elaine Hart
Fax: 071 928 1469
Telex: 8955803 SCLDNG

A comprehensive collection of engravings, illustrations and photographs, colour and b/w from 1842 onwards. Based on nine titles - The Illustrated London News, The Illustrated Sporting and Dramatic News, The Illustrated War News [1914-1918], The Graphic, The Sphere, The Tatler, The Bystander, The Sketch and Britannia and Eve - it is strong on all aspects of 19th and 20th Century history - social, industrial and political, Royalty, war, London, etc. Also the Thomas Cook Collection - a colourful travel archive of posters, brochure covers etc. c1840-1950. Brochures and rate card are available on request and visitors are welcome by appointment.
Quantity**** Format S Colour A-B-C-D B/W Illustration

The Image Bank
7 Langley Street, London WC2H 9JA
Tel: 071 240 9621-6
Contact: Mark Cass
Fax: 071 831 1489
Telex: 894839 TIB G

55 Spring Gardens, Manchester M2 2BX
Tel: 061 236 9226
Contact: Andrew/Rowan
Fax: 061 236 8723

Free 100pp catalogue available on request. One of the world's leading photo libraries, representing 650 photographers and illustrators from a network of 52 offices worldwide. Colour transparencies in all formats organised in over 800 categories including people (families, leisure, children), industry, scenic, travel, sports, agriculture, nature, animals, birds, food and special effects. For magazines, partworks and books (special price agreements available for regular users) please call our publishing department. Selections dispatched within hours. Visitors to our Covent Garden premises can assess our extensive, one million plus, file without any service fee. Complete subject list available. Clients in Liverpool and Manchester should use the new office in Manchester.
Quantity**** Format S Colour D Illustration

Images Colour Library Ltd
Kingswood House, 180 Hunslet Road, Leeds, West Yorkshire LS10 7AF
Tel: 0532 433389
Contact: Diana Leppard
Fax: 0532 425605

9 Rosemont Road, London NW3 6NG
Tel: 071 435 8175
Contact: Gary Fisk
Fax: 071 794 8853

Images is a general, contemporary library, specialising in top quality advertising, editorial and travel photography. Our stock is constantly being expanded and updated with new material commissioned specifically for the library market and available from our Leeds and London offices. Specialist photographers cover all the main stock categories and we have affiliations with top libraries around the world. Our free brochure pack is available on request. Visitors are welcome to our offices to make their own picture selections.
Quantity*** Format S/M/L Colour D

Impact Photos Ltd
26-27 Great Sutton Street, London EC1V 0DX
Tel: 071 251 5091
Contact: Hilary Genin
Fax: 071 608 0114

The Impact library features high quality colour and b/w editorial material, specialising in people and places with a strong emphasis on reportage. It covers a wide spectrum of subjects at home and abroad including politics, health, society, industry, sports, business, the environment, agriculture, and also Pamla Toler's specialist horticulture collection. Impact has a particularly strong reputation for world travel material, especially in developing countries. There are currently 125 contributing photographers but this is constantly expanding. A free colour brochure is available on request. Assignments are undertaken by our photographers.
Quantity**** Format S/M Colour D B/W

Imperial War Museum
Department of Photographs, Lambeth Road, London SE1 6HZ
Tel: 071 416 5000/5333
Contact: Jane Carmichael
Fax: 071 416 5374

A national archive of over 5 million photographs dealing with warfare in the 20th Century. The collection is mainly concerned with the two World Wars but also includes material on other conflicts involving the armed forces of Britain and the Commonwealth. The bulk of the collection is b/w but there are some colour transparencies (c1,500) dating from the Second World War and more is being acquired as the collection expands to cover more recent events such as the Falklands. The visitors room is open by appointment from Monday to Friday, 10 to 5. B/W prints are made to order (allow three weeks). Colour transparencies may be hired. Requests should be as specific as possible.
Quantity**** Format S/M//L Colour A-B-C-D B/W

The Independent Picture Library
Independent Newspapers, 40 City Road, London EC1Y 2DB
Tel: 071 956 1777
Contact: Liz Lynch
Fax: 071 962 0018

Since its launch in 1986, The Independent has been acclaimed for its use of b/w photographs. The Independent Picture Library is expanding rapidly and now contains over 100,000 images covering a wide range of subjects both domestic and foreign.
Quantity*** B/W

Innes Photographic Library
11-13 The Square, Hessle, N Humberside HU13 0AF
Tel: 0482 649271
Contact: Ivor Innes
Fax: 0482 647189

The library specialises, in depth, in its own location to include rural reference of East Yorkshire, Humberside and the Yorkshire and Lincolnshire Wolds. There is a unique and creative record of the construction and of the completed Humber Bridge. A b/w archive collection covers virtually the entire Hull based principal British deep water trawl fishing fleet and related topics from beginning to demise. Industrial and technological material, food, drink and cookery, sunsets, clouds and offshore and marine material, commercial and industrial requirements. Special requirements can be commissioned. Visits are most welcome.
Quanity*** Format S/M Colour C-D B/W

The Insight Picture Library
49 Bleaswood Road, Oxenholme, Kendal, Cumbria LA9 7EZ
Tel: 0539 740240/723391 (24 hrs)
Contact: Eddie Wren
Fax: 0539 730203

Insight started life as 'The Lake District Photo-Phile' and still specialises in that area, but now also has large and growing sections on three other major topics - wildlife, international travel and the police. In addition, Britain, including London, is well covered, especially northern England plus Devon and Cornwall and the whole of Scotland. Our location is not disadvantageous for deadlines. We frequently send material to London by Red Star in under 4 hours. Our team of over 60 photographers, based all over the world, is steadily growing in number. Enquiries from potential new contributors are welcome.
Quantity** Format S/M//L Colour D

International Photobank
Loscombe Barn Farmhouse, West Knighton, Dorchester, Dorset DT2 8LS
Tel: 0305 854145
Contact: Peter Baker
Fax: 0305 853065

A specialist library of travel pictures with worldwide coverage and British scenics in medium and large formats. There are over 180,000 transparencies as well as b/w prints in the collection. The photographs are of places, people, traditions, folklore and events around the world. Our British collection features stunning large formats of landscapes, towns, villages, historic castles and coastline.
Quantity*** Format M/L Colour C-D B/W Illustration

International Stock Exchange Photo Library
Raven House, 15-21 Cleveland Way, London E1 4TZ
Tel: 071 790 5560
Contact: Gaynor Lightfoot
Fax: 071 790 0001

The ISE Photo Library specialises in colour images of business and industry on a worldwide scale. Trading rooms, exchanges, business situations, cities, high tech, heavy industry, power, agriculture, transport, space, computer graphics... The library is also developing a general file with an emphasis on superb travel photography. The latest catalogue is free and gives a great introduction to a truly surprising source of high quality pictures, for use in brochures, books, magazines, advertising, presentations and so on.
Quantity** Format S/M Colour D

IPA Picture Library
c/o BAPLA, 13 Woodberry Crescent, London N10 1PJ
Tel: 081 444 7913
Fax: 081 883 9215

Extensive coverage over a wide range of topics concerning the Islamic world. Categories include religious, political, social and cultural events, conflicts, industry, communications, business, tourism, education, health, agriculture, dwellings, streets, cities, skylines, sport and recreation, people and personalities, architecture, art, calligraphy, crafts, flora, fauna and landscapes.
Quantity** Format S/M Colour C-D B/W

JAS Photographic

92/94 Church Road, Mitchum, Surrey CR4 3TD
Tel: 081 685 9593
Contact: Nick Holderness
Fax: 081 685 9479

The JAS Colour Air Photo Library has become by far the largest in the country, with extensive and continually updated blanket coverage of London, most counties, provincial towns, National Parks and the whole of Scotland at various scales from 1:2,5000 to 1:3,000 scale. Taken with large format mapping cameras (9" x 9") the photographs are extremely detailed to show a single building, a whole road or an entire town and are valuable for studying, recording and monitoring our environment. Flight indices are available upon request showing the location of each negative.
Quantity**** Format M/L Colour C-D

Camilla Jessel Photo Library

Riverside House, Riverside, Twickenham, Middx TW1 3DJ
Tel: 081 892 1470
Contact: Julie Stewart
Fax: 081 744 1217

A specialised archive of babies and children. Child development, psychological aspects as well as physical growth. Childbirth, newborns, children in hosptial, handicapped children and adults, socially disadvantaged children (UK, some Africa, South America), race relations and general relationships amongst various generations. Also child and adult musicians and the Royal Ballet on stage. 35mm colour and b/w.
Quantity** Formst S/M Colour C-D B/W

Joel Photographic Library

Unit 105 Blackfriars Foundry Annexe, 65 Glasshill Street,
London SE1 0QR
Tel: 071 721 7274
Contact: Patrick Skinner
Fax: 071 721 7276

A library established in 1988, stocking only originals to ensure optimum reproduction quality. General subjects are covered but not press or personalities. The fastest growing section is travel with a good selection of skies also available. If we cannot fulfill your request we will gladly consider shooting to your specific requirements and supplying material at stock prices. Commissions undertaken worldwide. Studio facilities available. Prompt, personal service strengthened by many years experience with advertising and editorials. Visitors welcome but please try to phone first.
Quantity** Form S/M Colour C-D

Patrick Johns

13 Woodberry Crescent, London N10 1PJ
Tel: 081 883 0083
Contact: Brian Shuel
Fax: 081 883 9215

A wide selection of horticultural subjects including cultural aspects of ornamentals and houseplants, lawns, fruit and vegetables, containers, pests, diseases, weed control and nutritional problems and practical step-by-step pictures of gardening operations. Complete subject list available of colour transparencies on 35mm and medium format and b/w prints. Assignments undertaken.
Quantity** Format S/M Colour C-D B/W

Katz Pictures Ltd

3-4 Kirby Street, London EC1N 8TS
Tel: 071 831 3370
Contact: Geoff Katz
Fax: 071 242 6638
Telex: 927960 KATZ UK G

This is an international agency with a constantly expanding library. We have a wide selection of contemporary show business personalities, general stock and serious reportage on a national and international scale. Our photographers include some leading London photojournalists available for reportage, studio and corporate assignments. We receive material from all over the world, including New York based JB Pictures, Matrix and Outline. We syndicate material from TV Guide, New Woman, Hello, Looks, Sunday Correspondent and Time Picture Syndication. We have a team of helpful researchers and you will find the agency friendly, enthusiastic and very active.
Quantity**** Format S/M Colour D B/W

The Kennel Club Library

1/5 Clarges St, London W1Y 8AB
Tel: 071 499 0844
Contact: Teresa Slowik
Fax: 071 495 6162

A specialist and expanding library covering many aspects of dogs and the dog world. Extensive coverage of personalities and people, dog shows, dog breeds, champions, veterinary science and field sports. The collection is mainly b/w and contains material dating back to c1870.
Quantity** B/W Illustration

The Keystone Collection

See **The Hulton Picture Company**

The Kobal Collection Ltd

4th Floor, 184 Drummond Street, London NW1 3HP
Tel: 071 383 0011
Contact: Dave Kent
Fax: 071 383 0044

The collection is one of the world's most valuable sources of film imagery, with over 750,000 colour and b/w photographs covering some 40,000 historic and modern film titles from around the world. The cinema has, since the early 1990's, covered almost all of mankind's activities, situations, moods and emotions. Our knowledgeable staff can quickly provide an apt image for the most abstract concept or for that elusive situational shot not available elsewhere. There is also an outstanding collection of portraits of the movie stars by leading Hollywood photographers such as Clarence Sinclair Bull, Ted Allan, George Hurrell, Ernest Bachrach, Ruth Harriet Louise and Lazlo Willinger.
Quantity**** Format S/M/L Colour A-B-C-D B/W

Kos Photos

4 Francis Gardens, Abbotts Meadow, Winchester,
Hampshire SO23 7HD
Tel: 0962 52107
Contact: Patrick Smart
Fax: 0962 55485

A colour library established in 1980 specialising in worldwide marine subjects from yacht racing to seascapes. With other 85,000 images and representing some of the best marine photographers in Europe and the US, Kos Photos is one of the more comprehensive libraries specialising in this area, with stock constantly increasing and being updated.
Quantity** Format S Colour D B/W

Lake District Photo-Phile

See **The Insight Picture Library**

Landscape Only
14a Dufours Place, London W1V 1FE
Tel: 071 734 7344/437 2655
Contact: Trevor Parr
Fax: 071 287 0126

As its name implies, a company which concentrates on landscape and related subjects in colour and b/w. Originally based on the work of Charlie Waite, it has expanded to include the work of other fine landscape photographers. A growing collection from all corners of the world with a strong emphasis on England and Europe.
Quantity Format S/M Colour D B/W**

Frank Lane Picture Agency Ltd
Pages Green House, Wetheringsett, Stowmarket, Suffolk IP14 5QA
Tel: 0728 860789
Contact: Jean Lane
Fax: 0728 860222

Established for over 40 years, this rapidly expanding library covers all aspects of natural history and weather. Representing some of the world's top photographers, the library has pictures suitable for both editorial and advertising use. Extensive colour and b/w coverage of mammals, birds, insects, fish and amphibians as well as dew, frost, snow, earthquakes, floods, glaciers, lightning, volcanoes, etc. The library works very closely with Eric and David Hosking and represents Silvestris Fotoservice from Germany.
Quantity* Format S/M Colour C-D B/W**

Andre Laubier Picture Library
4 St James Park, Bath, Avon BA1 2SS
Tel: 0225 420688
Contact: Andre Laubier

35mm and medium format photographs, illustrated maps, stereographs, posters, greeting cards dating from 1935 to the present day. Geography and UK travel, especially the West Country and Wales. France, Italy, Austria and Spain. Seasons, animals, birds, botany, agriculture, urban and country scenes, architecture, art and artists, industry, religion and religious architecture, transport, canals, sport, people, cutoms and crafts, abstracts and special effects. Researchers by appointment only. Stock lists on request. Photo assignments, artwork, design, line drawings undertaken with pleasure. English, French and German spoken (fluently).
Quantity Format S/M Colour A-C-D B/W Illustration**

Simon McBride Photographic Library
Unit 2B, 101 Farm Lane Trading Estate, London SW6 1JQ
Tel: 071 385 8112
Contact: Sandra Schadeberg
Fax: 071 381 0935
Telex: 265871 ref WQQ122

Simon McBride's original colour transparencies include mainly 35mm and some medium format. Comprehensive coverage of the landscape of England, Scotland and Wales, with the West Country in detail. Cities, towns, villages, some aerial shots and the landscape of major literary writers. Also gardens, wild and dried flowers. A new section in this library is a growing collection on Italy, since the photographer lives there. Photographic commissions undertaken.
Quantity Format S/M Colour D**

The MacQuitty International Photographic Collection
7 Elm Lodge, River Gardens, Stevenage Road, London SW6 6NZ
Tel: 071 385 6031/384 1781
Contact: Dr Miranda MacQuitty

250,000 colour and b/w photographs from the 1920's to the present day covering aspects of life in over 70 countries, people, customs, occupations, fishing, dancing, music, religion, funerals, archaeology, artefacts, art, crafts, museums, buildings, transport, surgery, acupuncture, food, drink, gardens, nature and scenery. Illustrated articles from the collection are circulated to 35 countries and the collection has produced 15 books. Brochure on request. Researchers welcome.
Quantity** Format S Colour A-B-C-D B/W**

Magnum Photos Ltd
2nd Floor, Moreland Buildings, 23/25 Old Street, London EC1V 9HL
Tel: 071 490 1771
Contact: Heather Vickers
Fax: 071 608 0020

Magnum was founded in 1947 by Cartier-Bresson, George Rodger, David Seymour and Robert Capa. Over 40 years, the agency has developed into the premier agency for photojournalists. There are now over 40 photographers working with Magnum worldwide. The library covers world events from the Second World War to the present day. In addition to unique social, economic and political coverage in virtually every country, the library also contains a vast personalities file: Monroe to Mitterand, Dean to Diana, Ghadafi to Geldfo. With helpful professional staff we aim to provide the best service to our clients along with what Magnum has always been renowned for - the best pictures.
Quantity** Format S/M/L Colour A-B-C-D B/W**

Mantis Studio Photographic Library
124 Cornwall Road, London SE1 8TQ
Tel: 071 928 3448
Contact: David Usill
Fax: 071 620 0350

Mantis specialises in off-beat travel photography. More than 40,000 colour transparencies cover the world from China to Sri Lanka, streets in Paris to temples in Bankok, sugar plantations in Cuba to Venezuelan rain forests and the Highlands of Scotland to the Berkshire countryside. These are not tourist pictures but a unique insight into the culture and the people who live there. If we don't have what you want, we will happily take it for you. Mantis Studio act as consultant designers to the Hot Air Balloon industry. Our own balloon is available for aerial photography and banner advertising.
Quantity Format S/M Colour D**

The Martin Library
45 Stainforth Road, Newbury Park, Ilford, Essex IG2 7EL
Tel: 081 590 4144
Contact: Frank Martin
Fax: 081 599 1166

A colour library of wildlife photographed by Frank Martin. Animals, birds, reptiles and insects from various parts of the world; India, Africa, the Americas, the Antarctic and Europe.
Quantity Format S Colour D**

S & O Mathews Photography
Stitches Farm House, Eridge, East Sussex TN3 9JB
Tel: 089 285 2848
Contact: Oliver Mathews
Fax: 089 266 5024

Library of colour transparencies of country life, landscapes, gardens and flowers.
Quantity Format S/M Colour C-D**

Microscopix Photolibrary
Middle Travelly, Beguildy, Nr Knighton, Powys LD7 1UW
Tel: 054 77 242
Contact: Andrew Syred

Microscopix is a photo library specialising in photomicrographs for technical, pictorial, educational and aesthetic purposes. Commissioned work of both biological or non-biological material may be undertaken, offering a wide variety of applicable microscopical techniques including the facility of low power stereoscopy. The film stock normally used is 35mm colour transparency on Kodak Ektachrome but monochrome or colour prints may be provided as preferred.
Quantity* Formst S Colour D

The Military Picture Library

TV House, 45a Whitemore Road, Guildford, Surrey GU1 1QU
Tel: 0483 573400
   0860 394580 mobile
Fax: 0483 573686

A specialist library covering in depth the British Army since 1971 as well as the TA and the Army Air Corps. Particular emphasis has been placed on men, uniforms and weapons - notably the latest small arms, artillery and tanks currently entering service. The logistics support that modern armies need has not been forgotten with engineers, transport, communications and other support roles covered. Recently, NATO forces have found a place in the library with BAOR and Soviet forces soon to feature. Commissioned military photography may also be undertaken by arrangement. 35mm, 6 ×6 and 5 ×4 transparencies as well as b/w prints available.
Quantity Format S/M Colour B-C-D B/W**

Millbrook House Picture Library

90 Hagley Road, Edgbaston, Birmingham B16 8YH
Tel: 021 454 1308
Contact: Patrick Whitehouse
Fax: 021 454 4224 (Millbrook Ho)

One of the largest specialist libraries dealing comprehensively with railway subjects worldwide, in colour and b/w. Subjects date from the turn of the century to the present day. Up to date material of UK, South America and the Far East especially China, but not Japan. Cities, rivers, bridges and general travel scenes. Also, England in the 1950's and 60's and a collection of steam and sail shipping. Mainly 35mm but some medium format. Rapid reply on availability. Orders dispatched same day. Clients welcome by appointment. The collection is ideal for books, magazines, advertising and calendars.
Quantity* Format S/M Colour A-B-C-D B/W Illustration**

Lee Miller Archives

Burgh Hill House, Chiddingly, Nr Lewes, East Sussex BN8 6JF
Tel: 0825 872 691
Contact: Anthony Penrose
Fax: 0825 872 733

The collected work of Lee Miller (1907-1977). 40,000 b/w negatives, 500 original prints. Main subject areas are: Surrealist and contemporary artists, poets and writers from the late 20's to 1970 including Aragon, Braque, Chadwick, Craxton, Delvaux, Dubuffet, Eluard, Ernst, Lam, Magritte, Man Ray, Moore, Miro, Penrose, Picasso, Steinberg, Tapies. Extensive studies of Egypt, the Middle East and the Balkans in the 30's, London during the Blitz, celebrities and fashion, War in Europe, siege of St Malo, liberation of Paris, Russian/American link-up at Torgau, fighting in Alsace, liberation of Dachau.
Quantity* B/W**

Monitor Syndication

17 Old Street, London EC1V 9HL
Tel: 071 253 7071
Contact: Davis Willis
Fax: 071 251 4405
Telex: 24718

This is an agency created by Monitor International and City Syndication merging. Monitor Syndication specialises in leading international personalities in colour and b/w. Politics, unions, business, stage and screen, pop, sports, law, the Royal Family - a large selection being added every day. Daily syndication to international, national and provincial media.
Quantity** Format S/M Colour B-C-D B/W**

Motoring Picture Library

National Motor Museum, Beaulieu, Hampshire SO4 7ZN
Tel: 0590 612345 ext 238
Fax: 0590 612624

Extensive library in colour and b/w covering the history of motoring from 1884 to the present day including cars, motorcycles, commercial vehicles and motorsport both past and present. Our photographers constantly travel the world to photograph cars and motorsport events for stock as well as carrying out commissions on behalf of advertising and editorial clients. We are agents for the Nicky Wright Collection, providing probably the largest selection of American cars outside the USA and new material arrives constantly. Same day dispatch. Researchers welcome. Brochure available on request.
Quantity** Format S/M/L Colour A-B-C-D B/W Illustration**

Moving Image Research and Library Services Ltd

21-25 Goldhawk Road, London W12 8QQ
Tel: 081 740 4606/4631
Contact: Michael Maloney
Fax: 081 749 6142

At Moving Image, thousands of images can be moving your way in a matter of minutes. The library, serviced by an expanding team of dedicated staff, is fully catalogued on a user friendly computer network. Each shot is carefully logged in great detail allowing instant access to the right material. For more information please call us at the numbers above. We look forward to your call.
Quantity* Format S/M/L Colour D

The Multi-Image Library

The Old School, Kingston St Michael, Nr Chippenham,
Wiltshire SN14 6JA
Tel: 0249 758187
Contact: Judy Roland
Fax: 0249 7582139

Compiled by audio-visual professionals for our industry's requirements and budgets. Includes *National Geographic* senior editor's pictures. Wide variety of subjects worldwide including all types of modern and historic transport, financial world, background graphics, textures and AV effects, architecture by building type, shopping, signs, food and drink, environments - urban, marsh, moor, mountain, etc. Locations worldwide include Madiera, Venice, The Algarve, Greece, UK, USA. Try us for unusual shots from octopi to vicars, wargames to craftsmen at work. Colour, mostly 35mm.
Quantity Format S Colour D**

David Muscroft Picture Library

Vision House, 16 Broadfield Road, Heeley, Sheffield S8 0XH
Tel: 0742 589299
Contact: David Muscroft
Fax: 0742 550113

The David Muscroft Picture Library is a specialist collection of images of snooker. Dating from the 19th Century and covering all aspects of the game in high quality colour and b/w. The collection is constantly being updated and expanded. We specialise in supplying large numbers of images for book publishers and packagers. Specific requests can be shot on commission. Material normally dispatched same day. We also hold a small, unique collection of pictures showing all aspects of Falkland Islands life from 1880 to the present day. This includes contemporary colour of a fast expanding economy.
Quantity Format S Colour D B/W**

Museum of Antiquities

Department of Archaeology, The University, Newcastle upon Tyne,
Tyne and Wear NE1 7RU
Tel: 091 222 7846/7844
Contact: Lindsay Allason-Jones
Fax: 091 261 1182
Telex: 53654 UNINEW G

The collection includes the Hadrian's Wall Archive: b/w photographs
(scenic views, excavations, etc) taken over the last 100 years, including
some J P Gibson. Also the Gertrude Bell Archive taken throughout the
Near East during her travels 1900-1926 and the Libyan Society
Archive. British material includes aerial photographs of
archaeological sites in Northumberland and Capability Brown
landscapes. Prehistoric, Roman, Anglo Saxon and Medieval artefacts
from the Museum of Antiquities, including famous items such as
Rothbury Cross and South Shields Bear Cameo. Visitors welcome and
enquiries cheerfully answered.
Quantity** Format S/M Colour D B/W

Museum of London Picture Library

150 London Wall, London EC2Y 5HN
Tel: 071 600 3699
Contact: Gavin Morgan
Fax: 071 600 1058

The history of London and its people from pre-history to the present
day. More than 500,000 photographs, mostly b/w covering the
topography, social and industrial history of London from 1840,
including rare collections such as the Port of London, Pavlova and
Suffragette collections. 15,000 negatives record paintings, prints,
drawings, costumes and other artefacts from the museum. The
archaeology collection includes 90,000 transparencies and b/w
negatives of excavations and associated finds from the London area
during the last 15 years. The Lord Mayor's Show recorded in detail
since 1982 is represented by more than 5,000 transparencies.
Quantity**** Format S/M/L Colour C-D B/W Illustration

NAAS Ltd (News Afro Asian Service)
See **Screen Ventures Ltd**

National Magazine Picture Library

72 Broadwick Street, London W1V 2BP
Tel: 071 439 5320/5000
Contact: S van Langenberg
Fax: 071 439 5007
Telex: 263879 NATMAG G

Syndication of photographs commissioned for their magazines. The
library includes a specialist computerised cookery section of pictures
from *Good Housekeeping* and a general selection of transparencies
covering fashion and beauty from *Harpers, Queen* and *Company*.
Also interiors and antiques. Material available for editorial use only
and occasional restrictions may apply since first option is given for in-
house magazine and book use. Visits by appointment only.
Quantity** Format S/M Colour C-D B/W Illustration

National Maritime Museum

Romney Road, Greenwich, London SE10 9NF
Tel: 081 312 6604
Contact: David Spence

The National Maritime Museum has over 3 million artifacts in the
collection including more than 3,000 oil paintings from the 17th to
20th Century, over 50,000 prints and drawings, copies of plans of
every ship built in the UK going back to the 17th Century, plus a huge
collection of navigational instruments, rare maps and charts,
manuscripts such as letters from Nelson and Pepys, ceramics,
weapons, uniforms, etc. The museum also houses a collection of more
than 300,000 historical photographs from 1840 to the present day.
Every maritime related subject is covered in the world's most
comprehensive Maritime Museum. As the Museum records these
items on film, more and more images are becoming available to the
general public and to commercial users.
Quantity**** Format L Colour B-C-D B/W Illustration

National Medical Slide Bank

Graves Medical Audiovisual Library, 220 New London Road,
Chelmsford, Essex CM2 9BJ
Tel: 0245 283351
Contact: Julie Dorrington
Fax: 0245 354710
Telex: 94012063 GMAL G

A specialist picture bank of over 10,000 transparencies of clinical and
general medicine with associated pathology and medical imaging,
drawn from collections of leading hospitals and medical schools in
the UK. The only collection of its kind, this picture bank has been
created specially to meet the needs of publishers, authors and
educators in the medical, nursing and general healthcare fields. The
bank has been established by Graves Medical Audiovisual Library, a
major supplier of a wide range of audiovisual materials for the
healthcare professions.
Quantity** Format S/M Colour A-B-C-D

National Monuments Record

Royal Commission on the Historical Monuments of England, Fortress
House, 23 Savile Row, London W1X 2JQ
Tel: 071 973 3091
Contact: Annie Woodward
Fax: 071 494 3998

The NMR, part of the Royal Commission on the Historical Monuments
of England (RCHME), is the national collection of photographs,
drawings and written records of archaeological sites and historic
buildings in England. The core of the collection is the RCHME's work
of survey and record carried out since 1908, supplemented by the
holdings of the original National Buildings Record, the Ordnance
Survey Archeology Division and the Department of the Environment's
library of air photographs. The archive is divided into three parts: the
National Buildings Record and the National Archeological Record in
London and the National Library of Air Photographs at Swindon.
Quantity**** Format S/M/L Colour A-B-C-D B/W

National Railway Museum

Leeman Road, York, North Yorkshire YO2 4XJ
Tel: 0904 621261
Contact: The Librarian
Fax: 0904 611112

The Library of the National Railway Museum holds outstanding
railway photography and railway poster collections. The
photographs range from official railway company views of
locomotives and carriages to amateur views of locomotives in action.
The number of negatives held totals some 250,000 and includes views
of railway air services, docks, ships and road vehicles as well as views
of locomotives and carriages. The poster collection contains 6,000
railway advertising posters dating from the late 19th Century to the
present day. Many of the images were commissioned from well-
known artists such as Norman Wilkinson, Frank Newbould, Tom
Purvis and Joan Hassall.
Quantity**** Format S/M Colour A-B-C B/W Illustration

The National Trust Photographic Library

39 Queen Anne's Gate, London SW1H 9AS
Tel: 071 222 9251/7690
Contact: Patrick Eaton
Fax: 071 222 5097

A library of colour transparencies covering all aspects of the Trust,
ranging from country houses and their interior decoration to beautiful
expanses of natural landscape and coastline in England, Wales and
Northern Ireland. Specialist collections of fine art, ceramics, furniture
and silver are exclusive to the library. Gardens, plant species, forests,
rural villages, dovecotes and mills protected by the Trust are
beautifully represented. The library offers an efficient dispatch and
follow-up service. We welcome researchers and our team of trained
staff can undertake telephone requests for pictures.
Quantity** Format S/M/L Colour D B/W

Natural Science Photos
33 Woodland Drive, Watford, Herts WD1 3BY
Tel: 0923 245265
Contact: Peter Ward
Fax: 0923 246067

A library of colour transparencies, mainly 35mm and some medium format, of a wide range of natural science subjects from many parts of the world, including animals, birds, reptiles, amphiba, fish, insects, terrestrial and aquatic invertebrates, habitats, plants and fungi. There is an extensive coverage of British botany and a growing collection of horticultural, ehtnic and freshwater angling photographs. Associated photographers, UK and overseas, subject to availability, will undertake commissions and speculative work. Applications for photographs may be made by phone or in writing. Visitors are welcome by appointment.
Quantity*** Format S/M Colour B-C-D

Nature Photographers Ltd
Ashley, Orchard Road, Basingstoke, Hants RG22 6NU
Tel: 0256 479617
Contact: Dr Paul Sterry
Fax: 0256 810880

Colour and b/w photographs of worldwide natural history and environmental subjects. We specialise in all aspects of British wildlife including birds, mammals, reptiles, amphibians, insects, plants, fungi and the sea shore. Our large collection of scenic shots are carefully sub-divided into region and habitat. The library also contains an extensive collection of African mammals, birds and scenics but our foreign coverage extends worldwide to include shots taken from the polar ice caps to the Amazon rainforests.
Quantity*** Format S/M Colour C-D B/W

Network Photographers
3-4 Kirby Street, London EC1N 8TS
Tel: 071 831 3633
Contact: Steve Mayes
Fax: 071 831 4468
Telex: 263484 NETWK

Network was founded in 1981 by a group of dedicated photojournalists and remains distinguished amongst British agencies as an organisation owned and directed by photographers with a sustained commitment to reportage. The Network archive is an extensive collection of images in both colour and b/w, fed by the continuing work of the photographers with current affairs, portraits and features from Britain and around the world. The accumulation of more than ten years photojournalism provides a huge stock resource as well as intelligent coverage of many specialist interests. All Network photographers are available for editorial and corporate assignments.
Quantity*** Format S/M Colour C-D B/W

Newsfocus Press Photograph Agency Ltd
18 Rosebery Avenue, London EC1R 4TD
Tel: 071 833 8691
Contact: David Fowler
Fax: 071 278 9180

Specialists in portrait photographs of leading British and International personalities, which are syndicated to the press, television and magazines. Photographs are in both 35mm colour and b/w and subjects covered include politics, entertainment, sport, media and Royalty.
Quantity* Format S Colour D B/W

NHPA
Little Tye, 57 High Street, Ardingly, Sussex RH17 6TB
Tel: 0444 892514
Contact: Tim Harris
Fax: 0444 892168

A comprehensive library of colour transparencies and b/w prints covering all aspects of the natural world. Active contributors from many countries provide a steady input of high quality pictures. As well as extensive files on mainstream flora and fauna, NHPA's archives contain much environmental, agricultural and scenic material. Specialisations include the unique high-speed photography of Stephen Dalton, the World of Shooting collection and unrivalled coverage by Peter Johnson and Anthony Bannister on African wildlife and the Kalahari Bushmen. UK agent for Australasian Nature Transparencies. Large studio available for commissions.
Quantity*** Format S/M/L Colour B-C-D B/W

The Northern Picture Library
Unit 2, Bentinick Street Industrial Estate, Ellesmere Street, Manchester M15 4LN
Tel: 061 834 1255
Contact: Roy Conchie
Fax: 061 832 6270

Colour transparencies in all formats. Landscapes and topographical photographs of British and world views. Also, general subjects: trees, animals, industry, farming, winter sports, seasons, sport, flowers. Poster available on request. Photographers available for commissions, possibly on a cost share basis.
Quantity*** Format S/M/L Colour B-C-D

Observer Colour Library
PO Box 33, Edenbridge, Kent TN8 5PB
Tel: 0342 850313
Contact: Alan M Smith
Fax: 0342 850244
Telex: 95351 TOPHAM G

Weekly since 1964, the *Observer Magazine* has created a very individual picture library. This collection of more than half a million outstanding pictures is now available for all media users from Topham Picture Source.
Quantity**** Format S/M Colour B-C-D

Only Horses Picture Agency
27 Greenway Gardens, Greenford, Middlesex UB6 9TU
Tel: 081 578 9047
Contact: Mike Roberts
Fax: 081 570 7595

A specialist library covering all aspects of the horse from foaling to retirement. Top action pictures taken at the Grand National, Derby, International Show Jumping and eventing here and abroad. Horse personalities, veterinary, breeds and polo. Photographs in colour and b/w available for editorial, commercial and advertising use.
Quantity*** Format S/M/L Colour B-C-D B/W

George Outram Picture Library
195 Albion Street, Glasgow G1 1QP
Tel: 041 305 3209
Contact: David Ball
Fax: 041 553 1355
Telex: 94018916

A comprehensive newspaper library of chiefly b/w photographs dating from c1900, serving the *Glasgow Herald* and *Evening Times*. Particular strengths are news, current affairs, Scotland, Glasgow, Clydeside, shipbuilding and engineering, personalities, World Wars One and Two and sport.
Quantity**** Colour D B/W

Oxford Scientific Films Ltd Photo Library

Long Hanborough, Oxford, Oxfordshire OX7 2LD
Tel: 0993 881881
Contact: Sandra Berry
Fax: 0993 882808
Telex: 83147 VIAOR OSF

Comprehensive coverage of natural history subjects photographed by Oxford Scientific Films. Also represents 200 wildlife photographers worldwide. 250,000 colour transparencies, some b/w prints and electron micrographs. Animals, plants, scenics, histology, embryology, conservation, ecological techniques, industry, technology, special effects, high-speed and time-lapse. UK agents for Animals Animals, New York. Photo features and illustrated articles supplied for UK and world markets. Assignment photography undertaken. Orders dispatched same day or clients welcome by appointment.
Quantity* Format S/M/L Colour C-D B/W**

Hugh Palmer

Knapp House, Shenington, Nr Banbury, Oxon OX15 6NE
Tel: 0295 87433
Contact: Hugh Palmer
Fax: 0295 87707

Photographer's growing collection of medium format garden pictures, amassed during numerous specialist commissions for books and magazines. Extensive coverage of Britain and an increasing number of European gardens. Practical gardening techniques, design ideas and plant types are included. Also represented in the collection are interior and exterior architectural shots from all parts of Britain - stately homes, country houses, conservatories and garden buildings.
Quantity* Format M Colour D

Panos Pictures

9 White Lion Street, London N1 9PD
Tel: 071 278 1111
Contact: Adrian Evans
Fax: 071 278 0345
Telex: 9419293 PANOS G

Documentary colour and b/w library specialising in Third World and Eastern European photography with an emphasis on environment and development. Important issues covered include: deforestation, desertification, erosion, pollution, agriculture, industry, ethnic, religion, housing, health and sanitation and all aspects of rural and urban life. Fast efficient service. Brochure available on request. All profits from the library are covenanted to the Panos Institute to further its international work in sustainable development.
Quantity Format S Colour D B/W**

David Paterson Library

88 Cavendish Road, London SW12 0DF
Tel: 081 673 2414
Contact: David Paterson
Fax: 081 675 9197

The David Paterson Library is a highly edited personal collection of photographs with a strong emphasis towards landscape and travel. The library has two specialities - Scotland and Nepal - with large collections of each in all formats. There are also selections on Donegal, the Falklands, France, Germany, Greece, Italy, Japan, London, the Malvern Hills, North West England, Oman and the Emirates, Portugal, Sicily, Shropshire and Herefordshire, Spain, Tenerife, Tunisia and Turkey. General subjects are also covered such as industry, nature and the environment, skies and weather effects.
Quantity Format S/M/L Colour C-D**

Penrose Pictures

Burgh Hill House, Chiddingly, Near Lewis, East Sussex BN8 6JF
Tel: 0825 872691
Contact: Tony Penrose
Fax: 0825 872733

All types of farming, rural life, forestry, flora and fauna. Also landscapes and places of historic interest, ethnic crafts, customs and costumes. Britain, Turkey, Afghanistan 1971, Iran 1971-77, India, Australia, New Zealand, Peru, Colombia, Equador, Central America, USA and Canada. Mainly 35mm, some b/w and colour negative.
Quantity Format S Colour C-D B/W**

The Photo Co-op

61 Webbs Road, London SW11 6RX
Tel: 071 228 8949
Contact: Janis Austin
Fax: 071 738 1462

Specialising in domestic social issues, the Photo Co-op is an expanding collection of contemporary material. Established in 1980, special areas of the collection in colour and b/w include babies and children, disablement, education, the elderly, the environment, family, health, housing and homelessness, industry, leisure, maternity, people, race, trade unions, unemployment, womens' issues and youth. A full list is available and the library is open weekdays from 9.30 - 5.30.
Quantity Format S/M Colour D B/W**

Photo Flora

46 Jacoby Place, Priory Road, Edgbaston, Birmingham B5 7UN
Tel: 021 471 3300
Contact: Andrew Gagg

An extensive and rapidly expanding specialised collection of colour transparencies of British and European wild plants. Thousands of subjects including virtually all the British species, rare and common, flowering plants, wild herbs, trees, shrubs, water plants, grasses, sedges and ferns, all accurately named, using up-to-date scientific and English nomenclature. Attractive coverage of each subject with pictures suitable for both popular and scientific applications. Habitat pictures also available. Applications for photographs may be by post or telephone and are normally dealt with by return. Full list on request.
Quantity Format S Colour C-D**

Photo Library International Ltd

PO Box 75, Leeds LS7 3NZ
Tel: 0532 623005
Contact: David Horgan
Fax: 0532 625366
Telex: 55293 Chamcon G/PLI

Comprehensive modern colour library servicing advertising, publishers, travel industry, calendar and greeting card companies, etc. Specialist subjects include various aspects of industry and Yorkshire views. Large format dupes supplied.
Quantity Format L Colour A-B-C-D**

Photo Resources

The Orchard, Marley Lane, Kingston, Canterbury, Kent CT4 6JH
Tel: 0227 830075
Contact: Michael Dixon
Fax: 0227 830075

Archaeology, art, ancient art, ethnology, history, mythology, world religion, museum objects, ancient warfare. Colour in 35mm and medium format and b/w.
Quantity Format S/M Colour C-D B/W**

The Photo Source

See **The Telegraph Colour Library Ltd**

Photofile International Ltd

Unit 2B, 101 Farm Lane Trading Estate, London SW6 1QJ
Tel: 071 385 8112
Contact: Sandra Schadeberg
Fax: 071 381 0935
Telex: 265871 ref WQQ122

Free, full colour catalogue available. Photofile represents an international group of advertising photographers who regularly shoot for the library to satisfy clients' requirements. Major areas of emphasis are people, families, couples, travel, sports, industrial and worldwide scenics. Clients are primarily advertising agents, graphic designers, travel tour operators, record companies, poster and calendar companies.
Quantity* Format S/M Colour D**

The Photographers' Library
81a Endell Street, London WC2H 9AJ
Tel: 071 836 5591/240 5554
Contact: Liz Higgins
Fax: 071 379 4650

The library has a large, constantly updated coverage of the principal European, Eastern European, North America, African and Far Eastern centres and areas. Most other favourite subjects such as industry, transport, sport, skiing, families, girls, scenics, sunsets and seascapes are also covered comprehensively. Orders are despatched the day they are requested or clients are welcome to undertake their own research. Free brochure available.
Quantity* Format S/M/L Colour C-D**

Photomotion
PO Box 605, Virginia Water, Surrey GU25 4SS
Tel: 0344 844430
Contact: Steven Behr
Fax: 0344 843513

Ever expanding action and travel-based collection; the action section contains largely snow-skiing and skiing related subjects and includes the work of several well known ski photographers but also includes a large mountain-biking section and other action sports. The comprehensive ski collection also covers people/apres ski and resort shots. Travel includes UK/Europe and a growing selection of worldwide destinations including the USA, Australia, New Zealand, Seychelles and Bali amongst others. Colour transparencies, mostly 35mm and some medium format. Commissions undertaken and complete ski/action shoots can be arranged to suit specific budgets. Ski/action models are also available.
Quantity* Format S/M Colour D

Photos Horticultural
169 Valley Road, Ipswich, Suffolk IP1 4PJ
Tel: 0473 257329
Contact: Michael Warren
Fax: 0473 233974

Horticultural pictures covering all aspects of gardening, including practical, plants and places to visit in both Britain and abroad. Commissions undertaken worldwide. Original colour transparencies in medium and large format. B/W supplied from colour through our own laboratories, which also offer a duplicating service.
Quantity Format M/L Colour B-C-D**

PictureBank Photo Library Ltd
Parman House, 30/36 Fife Road, Kingston upon Thames, London KT1 1SY
Tel: 081 547 2344
Contact: Martin Bagge
Fax: 081 547 2241
Telex: 8811940

Colour library with rapidly expanding stock. Major selection of girl photography of leading models, keep-fit beauty to nude, mostly medium or large format. Catering for magazine, calendar, travel, advertising, etc. Children, couples, families, for all requirements. European and world scenics, many on large format for jigsaws, the travel market, etc. Large London collection, extensive and mainly European hotel collection including people. Mood, animals, sport, technology and a growing collection of paintings. Library visits welcome. Photographers available for commission.
Quantity** Format S/M/L Colour D**

Picturepoint Ltd
Hurst House, 157-169 Walton Road, East Molesey, Surrey KT8 0DX
Tel: 081 941 4520
Contact: Ken Gibson
Fax: 081 979 6671

The Picturepoint collection has more than half a million high quality colour transparencies in all formats and of all subjects. Very strong on aviation, geographical, travel, Biblical, historical, fine art, food, antiques, people, sport, industry and agriculture. Also, a collection of early 20th Century advertising. The collection grows by more than 100 per month from the world's best freelance photographers. We relentlessly remove all the ancient, pink grotties from our files so that all our bright and colourful transparencies are matched only by our bright and cheerful welcome.
Quantity** Format S/M/L Colour B-C-D**

Pictures Colour Library Ltd
10a Neals Yard, Covent Garden, London WC2H 9DP
Tel: 071 497 2034
Contact: Michael Queree
Fax: 071 497 3070

Pictures is a leading London library, offering top quality images from photographers specialising in the following: landscapes, travel, people, children, food, interiors, architecture, glamour, industry and still life. We also have some computer graphics. Our transparencies are individually presented and are in all formats. The library is open for business from 9.30 to 5.30 and requests taken by phone are researched and dispatched the same day. Clients are most welcome to visit the library and carry out their own research. If you need more information, please ring us.
Quantity Format S/M/L Colour D**

Pink Shadow Picture Library
Ingulfs Cottage, Church End, Paglesham, Essex SS4 2DT
Tel: 0702 258965
Contact: David Saunders

This is a new general library with increasing stock levels on motor racing and drivers from 1967 to the present, a large selection of the finest steam train photography, glamour, wild birds and their nests and habitats, London at night, balloons, boating, canals and waterways, Middle Eastern and UK flowers, traction engines, animals, children, people, historic lantern slides, landscapes, seascapes and general travel. Colour transparencies in all formats. Same day service. Commissions undertaken - particularly motor sport.
Quantity Format S/M Colour D**

Pitkin Pictorials Ltd
ITPS Building, North Way, Andover, Hants SP10 5BE
Tel: 0264 334303
Contact: Shelley Grimwood
Fax: 0264 334110
Telex: 47214

This is an architectural library containing large format colour transparencies and b/w material which has been specially commissioned for the Pitkin Guides to cathedrals, churches and stately homes.
Quantity* Format L Colour C-D B/W

Planet Earth Pictures/Seaphot Ltd
4 Harcourt Street, London W1H 1DS
Tel: 071 262 4427
Contact: Jennifer Jeffrey
Fax: 071 706 4042

Worldwide marine and natural history photographs. All aspects of
the sea and man's involvement with it and a comprehensive collection
of underwater photographs. Marine photographs include seascapes,
marine animals and plants, underwater technology, oil production
and fishing. Wildlife from the poles to the tropics include mammals,
insects, birds, fish, reptiles, amphibians etc. Flowering and non-
flowering plants. Landscapes include mountains, deserts, icebergs,
space, coastlines, forests and rivers. Farming pollution, ecology.
Watersports, scuba diving, canoeing, hang gliding and windsurfing.
Commissioned photography and film production undertaken,
particularly underwater.
Quantity*** Format S/M/L Colour C-D

Axel Poignant Archive
115 Bedford Court Mansions, Bedford Avenue, London WC1B 3AG
Tel: 071 636 2555
Contact: Roslyn Poignant

Emphasis on anthropological and ethnographic subjects and also
natural history, landscape and aerial photography, particularly from
Australia and the South Pacific. Some European material, mainly
Sicily, England and the mythology and early history of Scandinavia.
Quantity** Format S/M Colour A-B-C-D B/W Illustration

Popperfoto
Paul Popper Ltd, 24 Bride Lane, Fleet Street, London EC4Y 8DR
Tel: 071 353 9665/6
Contact: Liz Moore
Fax: 071 936 2153
Telex: 8814206 Popper G

Popperfoto, credit line for **Reuter and UP(UK),** Agence-France
Presse and European Pressphoto Agency qv, Acme, INP, Planet, Paul
Popper, **Conway Picture Library** qv, Exclusive News Agency,
Odhams Periodicals Library, Illustrated, H G Ponting, Harris Picture
Agency, etc. Colour from 1940 and b/w from 1870 to the present.
Ponting's collection holds the Scott 1910-12 Antarctic expedition.
Major subjects include events and personalities - particularly World
War Two - Royalty, sport, politics, transport and crime, the history and
social conditions of countries all over the world, mainly 1930 to '60s
and '70s with updating where possible. The policy of Popperfoto is to
make material readily available, usually the same day, to publishers
and media throughout the world. Material is loaned and
reproduction fees charged.
Quantity** Format S/M/L Colour A-B-C-D B/W
Illustration**

Premaphotos Wildlife
2 Willoughby Close, Kings Coughton, Alcester, Warks B49 5QJ
Contact: Jean Preston-Mafham
Fax: 0789 400310

A collection of 35mm transparencies covering a comprehensive
range of animals and plants photographed in their natural
environments worldwide. Subjects include flowering and non-
flowering plants, fungi, slime moulds, fruits and seeds, galls, leaf
mines, seashore life, amphibians, reptiles, birds, mammals, molluscs,
crustaceans, insects, spiders and their allies, habitats and scenery. Also
a large selection of photographs of cultivated cactus. Commissions
undertaken and visitors welcome.
Quantity** Format S/M Colour C-D

Professional Sport
8 Apollo Studios, Charlton Kings Mews, London NW5 2SA
Tel: 071 482 2311
Contact: Tommy Hindley
Fax: 071 482 2441
Telex: 265871 MONREF G

Professional Sport is a constantly expanding library, established in
1977 and featuring the work of Tommy Hindley. The library covers all
aspects of sporting events and includes a specialist collection library
on tennis, dating back to the 18th Century. All major sporting events
worldwide are covered. 35mm and b/w prints are available for
editorial and commercial use.
Quantity**** Format S/M Colour C-D B/W

QA Photos Ltd
8 Stade Street, Hythe, Kent CT21 6BD
Tel: 0303 268223
Contact: Julian Glover
Fax: 0303 266273

QA Photos are the official photographers for Eurotunnel on the
Channel Tunnel Project and have been involved since the early days.
Thus the library has a large, increasing collection covering all facets
of the tunnel works, including those in France, plus many other aspects
of the project. The photographs are those which are valuable for
technical reasons as well as many which are visually interesting. Due
to the nature of the project, the stock is held principally on colour
negative film which produces exceptionally high quality prints or
transparencies. A significant stock of other material is available
covering Dover Harbour, cross-channel ferries and other transport
and maritime subjects.
Quantity*** Colour D

Quadrant Picture Library
Quadrant House, The Quadrant, Sutton, Surrey SM2 5AS
Tel: 081 661 8888
Contact: Elaine Jones
Fax: 081 661 8933
Telex: 892084 REEDBP G

A collection of colour on 35mm and medium format and b/w
covering all aspects of transport and motorsports from the early
years of the century to the present day. Included are cars, commercial
vehicles, bicycles, aeroplaces, motor boats, yachts and trains. Material
is produced by the journals of Reed Business Publishing Ltd. Also
included is a collection of motoring artwork from the 1920's and 30's
which is available on transparency.
Quantity**** Format S/M Colour C-D B/W Illustration

Railways and Steam Locomotives of the World
The Square, Newton Harcourt, Leicestershire LE8 0FQ
Tel: 053759 2068
Contact: Diana Wisden

Twenty years ago, Colin Garratt devoted his life to documenting
professionally the last working steam locomotives of the world. His
pictures are known internationally for their beauty and range of
expressions - every mood, colour and location to provide the
definitive source of images for every conceivable use. Already he has
covered some fifty countries but his global quest proceeds apace
providing a continuous source of exciting, fresh material of both
steam and modern railways. The library also contains the work of
other leading railway photographers including Dr Bill Sherman's
celebrated collection of famous trains, tourist/preserved railways and
modern traction. Brochure available.
Quantity** Format S/M Colour A-B-C-D B/W Illustration

Redferns
7 Bramley Road, London W10 6SZ
Tel: 071 792 9914
Contact: David Redfern
Fax: 071 792 0921

Established in 1960, the library covers the world of popular music, jazz, rock and pop, easy listening, heavy metal, country and folk, in colour and b/w. Over 3,000 artists are represented. Included is a unique, early American jazz collection. Other subjects include discos, musical equipment, recording studios, crowds, etc. Full list is available.
Quantity** Format S/M Colour B-C-D B/W**

Reflex Picture Agency Ltd
See **Impact Photos Ltd**

Relay Photos Ltd
2 Queensborough Mews, London W2 3SG
Tel: 071 402 2178
Contact: Andre Csillag
Fax: 071 706 4564

Comprehensive library of colour and b/w pictures covering pop music personalities of the last 20 years. Library constantly updated from work undertaken worldwide. Supplying pictures for promotional material, tour books, record companies and magazines, etc. and covering all aspects of the rock industry.
Quantity** Format S Colour B-C-D B/W**

Remote Source Photographic Library
1 Kensington Gore, London SW7 2AR
Tel: 071 589 5466
Contact: Rachel Duncan
Fax: 071 581 9918
Telex: 933669 RGS LDN

This is a unique directory and stock library of expedition photographs from remote, unusual and adventurous destinations. Our principal emphasis is on the places, people and culture of wilderness areas worldwide, with particular reference to arduous and adventurous activities. In addition, we maintain an accurate schedule of current and planned expeditions, have extensive, regular contact with expedition leaders and photographers and, with prior knowledge, can arrange for specific shots to be commissioned. Direct or remote source, we will locate your picture needs.
Quantity Format S Colour D B/W**

Repfoto London
74 Creffield Road, Acton, London W3 9PS
Tel: 081 992 2936
Contact: Robert Ellis
Fax: 081 992 9641

Specialists in rock, pop, folk and jazz music and musicians. The library consists of colour on 35mm and medium format and b/w photographs of musicians performing, backstage, on the road and in the photo studio, on location, in the recording studio, at festivals. Particularly strong on rock and heavy metal subjects from the late '60s to date.
Quantity Format S Colour B-C-D B/W**

Retna Pictures Ltd
1 Fitzroy Mews (off Cleveland St), London W1P 5DQ
Tel: 071 388 3444
Contact: Anne Holley
Fax: 071 383 7151

An extensive library of colour transparencies in all formats and b/w prints, representing a large number of top class photographers. The library specialises in high quality portraits and performance shots of international rock and pop personalities, actors and actresses, entertainers and celebrities. We can also provide material from our general stock library which covers an increasing range of subjects including travel, flora and fauna, people, the environment, sport and leisure, etc. Offices in New York and Los Angeles and associated agencies worldwide. Colour brochure available. Personal callers welcome.
Quantity** Format S/M/L Colour A-B-C-D B/W**

Retrograph Archive Ltd
164 Kensington Park Road, Notting Hill Gate, London W11 2ER
Tel: 071 727 9378/9426/6422(24 hr)
Contact: J Ranicar-Breese
Fax: 071 229 3395

A vast archive of commercial and decorative art (1860-1960). Worldwide labels and packaging for food, wine, chocolate, soap, perfume, cigars and cigarettes. Fine art and commercial art journals, fashion magazines, posters, Victorian greeting cards, wallpaper and gift wrap sample books, music sheets, folios of decorative design and ornament - Art Nouveau and Deco - hotel, shipping and airline labels, memorabilia, tourism, leisure, poster art, postcards, food and drink, transport and entertainment. Suitable for books, cards, calendars, gift and social stationery, compact discs. Original viewed then photographed to order. Lasers for book dummies, packaging mock-ups, film and TV action props. Brochure on request.
Quantity** Format M Colour D B/W Illustration**

Reuter and UPI (UK)
Available from **Popperfoto,** 24 Bride Lane, Fleet Street, London EC4Y 8DR
Tel: 071 353 9665/6
Contact: Liz Moore
Fax: 071 936 2153
Telex: 8814206 POPPER G

Daily news coverage on international events, taking in around 90-150 b/w pictures daily. Subjects include international politics, wars, disasters, Royalty, personalities and worldwide news events. Photos are transmitted from the ends of the Earth, so there is no waiting for planes to arrive. Popper have been the UK agents for UPI for many years and Reuters since the photo service started in 1985. The UPI collection includes Planet News and commences mid 1920's continuing, largely complete, through to today's news photos.
Quantity** B/W**

Rex Features Ltd
18 Vine Hill, London EC1R 5DX
Tel: 071 278 7294/3362 (Library)
Contact: Paul Brown
Fax: 071 837 4812
Telex: 25491 REXPHO G

Comprehensive colour - 35mm and some medium format - and b/w library established in the early 1950s. Constantly expanded stock includes national and international news, politics, personalities, show business, rock and pop, glamour, animals both humerous and scientific, art, medicine, science, situations and landscapes. Specialities include current affairs, off-beat and amusing pictures, candid and studio celebrities and British and foreign Royalty. Many renowned photographers are represented. Pictures readily available both individually and as features with quick access via a fully computerised system.
Quantity** Format S/M/L Colour A-B-C-D B/W Illustration**

Ann Ronan Picture Library
Wheel Cottage, Bishops Hull, Taunton, Somerset TA1 5EP
Tel: 0823 252737
Contact: Ann Ronan
Fax: 0823 336785

History of science and technology: 150,000 illustrations, mainly from printed sources from AD 1500-1920, including personalities, scientific experiments, manufacturing processes, mining, agricultural practices, transport, working and living conditions, child labour, cookery, communications, recreations, medicine, etc. Approximately 7% in colour. Original material not loaned but supplied as b/w prints or colour transparencies.
Quantity* Illustration**

RoSPA
Cannon House, The Priory, Queensway, Birmingham B4 6BS
Tel: 021 200 2461
Contact: Joan Chesterton
Telex: 336546

A varied collection of colour transparencies and b/w prints covering all aspects of safety and its environment. Road safety includes pedestrians, cyclists, HGVs, roads and street furniture. Occupational safety includes industrial transport, industry, factories, offices, people at work and accidents. Home and leisure safety includes sport, gardening, accidents in the home and care of the elderly and the young. Water safety includes rivers, canals and the sea. Also safety education - schools, teachers, playgroups, police and the fire service.
Quantity Format S/M Colour C-D B/W**

Royal Air Force Museum
Grahame Park Way, Hendon, London NW9 5LL
Tel: 081 205 2266 ext 208
Contact: David Ring
Fax: 081 200 1751

The photographic collection records the history of military aviation from its earliest days to the present. The development of aircraft is covered both at home and overseas, from balloons to space flight. The majority of the collection is black and white. Some colour photographs are available from World War Two to the present. All formats are available and copies can be supplied. The museum also owns the Charles E Brown Collection. The Reading Room can be used by prior appointment Monday-Friday, 10 - 4.30. Limited research will be carried out and search fees will be charged.
Quantity* Format S/M/L Colour A-B-C-D B/W**

Royal Geographical Society Picture Library
1 Kensington Gore, London SW7 2AR
Tel: 071 589 5466
Contact: Rachel Duncan
Fax: 071 581 9918
Telex: 933669 RGS LDN

This is the focal point for British geographical and exploration activity. The strength of the picture library lies in some 100,000 b/w prints and negatives dating from the 1860's to the middle of this century. Some of the more notable collections included are the expeditions of Scott and Shackleton to Antarctica and British Everest expeditions, including the first successful ascent in 1953. There are also a number of drawings and fine paintings. The modern collection of 35mm transparencies include recent RGS expeditions to remote parts of the world.
Quantity* Format S/L Colour A-B-C-D B/W Illustration**

Royal Photographic Society
The Octagon, Milsom Street, Bath, Avon BA1 1DN
Tel: 0225 462841
Contact: Deborah Ireland
Fax: 0225 488688

This collection of over 80,000 images covers the history and progress of photography. The subject emphasis is pictorial and photography as an art rather than documentary record, though there are exceptions. Dating from 1827 with heliogravures by Niépce, the collection is represented by all legendary photographers from both sides of the Atlantic, is largely donated and represents the photographer rather than the subject. There are substantial holdings on portraiture, 19th Century landscapes, architecture, India, Victorian rural life, etc. Staff are happy to help with queries about more esoteric subject matter. 15,000 b/w images arranged in an alphabetical index make subject searching relatively easy. Prints are available and other material can be copied on request. Visits by appointment only, Monday to Friday, 10-5. Charges depend on degree of staff involvement.
Quantity* B/W**

RSPB Photolibrary
The Lodge, Sandy, Bedfordshire SG19 2DL
Tel: 0767 680551
Contact: Chris Sargeant
Fax: 0767 692365

From a solitary Goldcrest to 30,000 pink-footed geese at the Loch of Strathbeg. The RSPB is Europe's largest voluntary conservation organisation and the Society's photo library reflects the scope of our conservation effort. 25,000 colour transparencies in all formats and 15,000 b/w prints representing 60 photographers - and expanding. Subjects include British wild birds, RSPB nature reserves, habitats and land management, environmental threats, practical conservation work, birdtables and feeders, birdwatching activities, oil pollution. All profits directed to RSPB's Action for Birds campaign. Visitors by appointment please.
Quantity Format S/M/L Colour D B/W**

S & G Press Agency Ltd
68 Exmouth Market, Clerkenwell, London EC1R 4RA
Tel: 071 278 1223
Contact: Paul Kurton
Fax: 071 278 8480

Sport and General is one of the oldest press photo libraries in Britain. The library has more than 300,000 colour transparencies and over 1,000,000 b/w negatives reflecting each decade of this century. As the name suggests, we are a specialist sports library but we also have a vast collection of news, personality and Royalty photographs. Opening hours are 9 to 6. Requests can be made by phone or letter and the library is open for clients who would like to do their own research.
Quantity** Format S/M Colour A-B-C-D B/W**

Science Photo Library Ltd
112 Westbourne Grove, London W2 5RU
Tel: 071 727 4712
Contact: Michael Marten
Fax: 071 727 6041

The world's leading source of imagery on all aspects of science, technology and medicine. Top quality colour and b/w pictures on 35mm and medium format. Spectacular abstract, specialist and false-colour images. Fast, expert service, detailed captions. Laboratories, hospitals, industry, technical, and medical pictures. Astronomy, biology and biotechnology, botany, chemistry, computers and computer graphics, earth sciences and terrestrial phenomena, genetics, landscapes, medicine and physiology, physics, satellite imagery, scientific illustrations and artworks, spaceflight, technology and zoology. Free 48pp colour brochure available.
Quantity* Format S/M Colour C-D B/W Illustration**

Screen Ventures Ltd
49 Goodge St, London W1P 1FB
Tel: 071 580 7448
Contact: Michael Evans
Fax: 071 631 1265
Telex: 8951182 GECOMS

Extensive collection in colour and b/w of Asia, the Middle East and Northern Africa. Coverage includes every aspect of life in these areas: cultural, everyday scenes, landmarks, customs, the arts, technology, education, leisure, industry, agriculture, politics, religion and religious activities and personalities. Specialised knowledge and latest back-up information may be provided when requested. Commissions undertaken in the areas covered.
Quantity Format S Colour C-D B/W**

Sealand Aerial Photography
Goodwood Airfield, Chichester, West Sussex PO18 0PH
Tel: 0243 781025
Contact: Malcolm Knight
Fax: 0243 531422

Comprehensive colour aerial photographic coverage of subjects throughout the UK. We operate all through the year, utilising our own aircraft. The library contains over 400,000 negatives and transparencies on medium format. All applications of aerial photography are covered and rapid searches can be made through our computer data-base system.
Quantity** Format M Colour D**

Sefton Photo Library
30 Mason Street, Manchester M4 5EY
Tel: 061 832 7670/834 9423
Contact: Sefton Samuels
Fax: 061 834 9423

Wide selection of general subjects: sport, farming, sunsets, historic transport, animals, personalities, pictorial and practical photographs for advertising and publishing. Range of industrial subjects including oil rigs and refineries, foundries and sewage works, aircraft manufacture and general views. Our speciality is coverage of all aspects of the North of England and Wales as well as other areas of Britain and abroad. Authentic collection of Victorian and Edwardian scenes. Colour on 35mm and medium format and b/w.
Quantity* Format S/M Colour C-D B/W**

Select Photo Agency & Picture Library
B2 Studio Metropolitan Wharf, Wapping Wall, London E1 9SS
Tel: 071 265 1422
Contact: Shirley Berry
Fax: 071 265 1421
Telex: 8591182 GECOMS G

Select is a young news and current affairs agency with an accent on the three Es - Economy, Environment and the EEC. It also syndicates features and travel material. Select has close ties with REA in Paris, Contrasto in Rome and Milan, Saba Photos in New York and Cover in Madrid. These five agencies work exclusively for each other and hold each others' material on file. Select expands weekly and its photographers travel on commission worldwide. Commissions undertaken at short notice and Contrasto, REA, Saba and Cover photographers can be commissioned through Select. Researchers are always welcome.
Quantity* Format S/M Colour D B/W**

Phil Sheldon Golf Picture Library
3 Grimsdyke Crescent, Arkley, Barnet, Herts EN5 4AH
Tel: 081 440 1986
Contact: Karina Hoskyns
Fax: 081 440 9348

The golf picture library comprises over 150,000 colour and b/w photographs dating from 1976, including detailed coverage of many major championships, several Ryder Cup matches and over 250 other golf tournaments. This expanding collection also includes player action, portraits, instruction material, trophys and more than 150 golf courses from around the world.
Quantity* Format S Colour C-D B/W**

Brian and Sal Shuel
13 Woodberry Crescent, London N10 1PJ
Tel: 081 883 0083
Contact: Brian Shuel
Fax: 081 883 9215

The founding part of **Collections** qv, consisting of British traditional customs, British bridges, a sizable file on London and a miscellany of black and white fun. The custom files, covering over 200 subjects and including old illustrations, developed from a b/w project on the 'folk revival' in the sixties, with the earliest pictures of some now famous performers. The 350 bridges include every type from the pre-historic 'clam' bridges to the latest in pre-stressed concrete. The black and white is the result of 30 years of professional work as well as 30 years of sheer pleasure in photography.
Quantity* Format S/M Colour B-C-D B/W Illustration**

Anthea Sleveking
13 Woodberry Crescent, London N10 1PJ
Tel: 081 883 0083
Contact: Brian Shuel
Fax: 081 883 9215

A major part of **Collections** qv, consisting of over 15,000 transparencies on 35mm and medium format, specialising in human relationships from pregnancy, through birth, babies, child development, education, health and family life to old age. The collection was re-edited in 1990 but continues to grow. Commissions are welcomed - many have been carried out for the World Health Organisation and for a number of books, notably Dr Miriam Stoppard's definitive New Baby Care Book published in 1990. An interesting b/w collection of sixties portraits includes famous actors and authors and Sir Winston Churchill.
Quantity Format S/M Colour B-C-D B/W**

Skishoot-Offshoot
62 Roupell Street, London SE1 8SS
Tel: 071 620 0882
Contact: Felice Eyston
Fax: 071 928 7075

Skishoot is Britain's specialist ski picture library. More than 20,000 colour transparencies feature every aspect of the sport from action, ski surfing, hang-gliding and children to fashion, beauty, apres ski, snowscapes and resorts. All pictures taken by our own staff photographers based in the Alps and Colorado all winter - on European glaciers all summer. We will also shoot for you on location or in our London studio. Offshoot is a travel picture library specialising in America. New York, New Orleans, Houston, Los Angeles, San Fransisco, Virginia, Colorado, New Mexico, Arizona. Also material on Italy, England, Australia, Far East.
Quantity Format S/M Colour D B/W**

Skyscan Balloon Photography
Stanway Grounds, Stanway, Cheltenham, Glos GL54 5DR
Tel: 0242 621357 (24hrs)
Contact: Brenda Marks
Fax: 0242 621471

A unique collection of aerial views of Britain taken from a camera platform suspended beneath a tethered balloon. Cameras are remotely controlled by a ground operator and flown at heights of 50' to 500' - lower and closer to the subject than aircraft. A TV link allows precise composition and the vibration free system results in high quality images. The collection ranges from industrial and city scenes to open countryside and coastal views with an emphasis on landscape, stately homes and heritage sites. Transparencies, colour negative and b/w on medium format. Commissions undertaken, also infra-red and thermographic aerial surveys.
Quantity Format M Colour D B/W**

South American Pictures
48 Station Road, Woodbridge, Suffolk IP12 4AT
Tel: 03943 3963/3279
Contact: Marion Morrison
Fax: 0394 380176

Marion and Tony Morrison offer more than 75,000 colour and 20,000 b/w images of South America and Mexico. The collection is backed by 25 years' experience of film-making, travel and writing about South America. Almost every topic is covered with some, including archaeology and the Amaxon, extensively represented. Complementing the pictures, an extensive library of information is frequently updated by associates based in Latin America. A rapidly growing part of the library is the archival section, with pictures and documents from most countries.
Quantity* Format S/M Colour B-C-D B/W**

Space Frontiers Ltd
The Telegraph Colour Library Ltd, Unit C1, Enterprise Business Estate,
Mastmaker Rd, 2 Mill Harbour E14 9TE
Tel: 071 987 1212
Contact: Mike Watson
Fax: 071 538 3309
Telex: 888258

Specialist library of still and movie images derived from the US
manned and unmanned space programme - rocket launches, deep
space and orbital views of the Earth and its regions, including the UK,
men and machines in 'free' space and on the moon, spacecraft
images of sun and planets, computer enhancements, images of
spacecraft and a large selection of space shuttle material. Images of
Earth from British, European and Japanese resource centres and
space agencies. Pictures of constellations and telescope views of
comets, planets, galaxies and nebulae. Space art. Earth surface/
weather pictures of natural phenomena. Technical consultancy and
editorial service on these subjects from H J P Arnold on 0705 475313.
Quantity Format S/M/L Colour A-B-C-D B/W**

Spectrum Colour Library
146 Oxford Street, London W1N 9DL
Tel: 071 637 1587
Contact: Keith Jones
Fax: 071 637 3681

Suites 3 & 4, 7/8 Mill Hill, Leeds, West Yorkshire LS1 5DQ
Tel: 0532 445255
Contact: Peter Dransfield
Fax: 0532 425474

A large general library of modern, selectively edited transparencies
suitable for advertising or editorial use. We handle the work of over
600 international photographers and more than 30 corresponding
worldwide photo libraries. The north of England is serviced by our
Leeds office at 7-8 Mill Hill, Leeds LS1 5DQ Telephone 0532 445225
Fax 0532 425474 and our Barcelona office will open shortly. Our
colour catalogue is free to professional photography buyers. We
offer fast and friendly service.
Quantity** Format S/M/L Colour C-D B/W**

Split Second
1a Doughty Street, Grays Inn Road, London WC1N 2PH
Tel: 071 831 4316
Contact: Leo Mason
Fax: 071 831 4322

Leo Mason specialises in sports and live action with a very high
creative bias and is available for directly commissioned work. In
addition, Split Second has a very comprehensive selection of original
colour transparencies on 35mm and medium format, all of which can
be viewed at the office or sent upon request.
Quantity** Format S Colour C-D**

Frank Spooner Pictures Ltd
Room B7, Halton Square, 16-16a Baldwins Gardens,
London EC1N 7US
Tel: 071 405 9943
Contact: Mike Soulsby
Fax: 071 831 2483

In addition to British news coverage, this agency handles the
distribution in the UK of pictures from Gamma Presse Images of Paris
and Gamma Liaison in New York, whose photographers cover the
world. Most subjects including war, fashion, politics, travel, adventure,
tennis, yachting, glamour, animals, personalities, films and a host of
others, can be found in our extensive libraries in London, Paris and
New York. Contained in these three libraries there are 8,000,000
photographs, the work of 1,700 photographers. The libraries are
computerised and an expert staff can handle requests quickly. Colour
and b/w.
Quantity** Format S Colour B-C-D B/W**

Sporting Pictures (UK) Ltd
7a Lambs Conduit Passage, Holborn, London WC1R 4RG
Tel: 071 405 4500/1844
Contact: Steve Brown
Fax: 071 831 7991
Telex: 27924

Professional, amateur and leisure sports covered by our specialist
photographers result in a comprehensive library of over 3 million
colour and b/w pictures of major sporting names and events
throughout the world over the last fifteen years. Researchers are
welcome in the library, as are requests for pictures by phone. All
assignments undertaken on request.
Quantity** Format S Colour C-D B/W**

Still Pictures
199a Shooters Hill Road, Blackheath, London SE3 8UL
Tel: 081 858 8307
Contact: Susan Glen
Fax: 081 858 2049

Still Pictures is an environmental picture agency and library founded
by Mark Edwards. It contains a large selection of colour and b/w
images covering a wide range of environmental and development
issues from around fifty countries. The pictures have been taken over
the past twenty years and form an unique archive and pictorial
commentary on the state of the world's environment in all spheres,
reflecting the complexity of the problems and the solutions. Subjects
covered are urban and rural communities, industry and agriculture,
deforestation, erosion, pollution and waste, education, etc.
Quantity Format S Colour B-C-D B/W**

Stockphotos, Inc
3rd Floor, 7 Langley Street, London WC2H 9JA
Tel: 071 240 7361
Contact: Neil Andrews
Fax: 071 831 1489
Telex: 894839 TIB G

Call for our latest 80pp catalogue featuring the work of leading
international and UK photographers covering a broad range of
subjects including people, families, couples, executives, scenics,
industry, sport and leisure, travel, medical, food and drink and special
effects. Visit our Covent Garden offices, receive prompt, efficient
attention from our team of experienced researchers and see why
Stockphotos is one of the fastest growing libraries in the UK. Ask for
our free library subject list.
Quantity* Format S/M/L Colour D**

Tony Stone Worldwide Photolibrary
116 Bayham Street, London NW1 0ER
Tel: 071 267 8988
Contact: Jackie Lancaster
Fax: 071 722 9305

A free catalogue - available on request - provides an introduction to
an exclusive file of colour photography by leading professionals,
taken specially for books, magazines, partworks, AV, advertising,
corporate promotions, record sleeves, etc. This is a large general
library of international interest which includes specialist collections of
travel, wildlife, industry, sports, people and human relationships and
historic transport. TSW provides access to major editorial collections
of Americana and French life and culture in its subsidiaries in the USA
and France and provides access as well to miscellaneous collections
housed in its other offices.
Quantity** Format S/M/L Colour D**

Jessica Strang Ltd
86 Cambridge Gardens, London W10 6HS
Tel: 081 969 7292
Contact: Jessica Strang

The photographs cover a wide range of subjects but have a special interest in design, so countries tend to feature architectural detail, sculpture, markets and local colour rather than tourism. Countries include Bali, Malaysia, Singapore, Burma, Australia, America, Kenya, Sicily, Corsica, Spain, Holland and France. The bulk of the collection however is on current architecture and interior design, mainly domestic. Also designers', architects' and artists' homes together with their idiosyncratic collections and work. Special collections: greening the cities and minimal gardens, domestic recycling, working men and women as objects and the vanishing architectural detail of London.
Quantity** Format S Colour C-D

Survival Anglia Photo Library
48 Leicester Square, London WC2H 7FB
Tel: 071 321 0101
Contact: Sue Harrison
Fax: 071 493 2598
Telex: 299689

The library has grown up over the many years that the award-winning Survival programme has been on the ITV network. It is now an outstanding collection of natural history photographs by some of the world's top wildlife photographs. From pole to pole, on land, underwater and in the air, all aspects of natural history are covered, mostly on 35mm and some medium format colour transparencies plus b/w prints. Free subject catalogue on request.
Quantity*** Format S/M Colour B-C-D B/W

Swift Picture Library
Claremount, Redwood Close, Ringwood, Hants BH24 1PR
Tel: 0425 478333
Contact: Mike Read
Fax: 0425 471525
Telex: 41601 GRAYBH G

Specialists in nature and scenic photography. Colour transparencies on 35mm and medium format. Our collection of scenics is heavily biased towards Britain but West Greenland and parts of Africa are also covered. Scenics cover a wide variety ranging from wild landscapes, moody compositions and country scenes to aerial views, urban scenes and city studies. Natural history subjects are widely covered by portraits, close-ups, action and behavioural shots of birds, mammals, reptiles, amphibians, fishes, insects and other invertebrates, plants and fungi, etc. Commissions undertaken. Visitors by appointment.
Quantity*** Format S/M Colour B-C-D

Sygma Ltd
Wheatsheaf House, 4 Carmelite Street, London EC4Y 0BN
Tel: 071 353 4551/2/3
Contact: Helen Finney
Fax: 071 583 4239

On April 1st 1990, Sygma opened its own London office to provide a comprehensive stock library to its customers, as well as its specialist collections. Sygma's strength is in showbiz material by top-name photographers such as Douglas Kirkland, Helmut Newton, Eddie Adams and Bettina Rheims; first-class news coverage from around the world; in-depth features which stand independent of copy; personalities from all walks of lilfe and extensive historical material from the archives of L'Illustration and Keystone. Sygma's aim is to provide you with what you need as quickly as possible from the London library or the extensive resources in the Paris-based head office.
Quantity**** Format S Colour A-B-C-D B/W

Syndication International Ltd
4-12 Dorrington St, London EC1N 7TB
Tel: 071 404 4459
Contact: Joanna Holmberg
Fax: 071 430 2437
Telex: 267503 SYNINT G

A general agency handling syndication of photographs and text from Mirror Group Newspapers and also acting for numerous freelance photographers. The library holds colour in all formats and b/w prints on a variety of subjects but with an emphasis on personalities, Royalty, news, sport, animals, cookery, beauty and crime. The Britain in Pictures collection is held here, also the Picturegoer Collection and Financial Times Computer Graphics.
Quantity**** Format S/M L Colour C-D B/W Illustration

Telefocus
Room A381, British Telecom Centre, 81 Newgate Street,
London EC1A 7AJ
Tel: 071 356 6591/2/3
Contact: Philip Green
Fax: 071 606 1179

Our comprehensive collection of telecommunication photographs covers a wide range of subjects from optical fibres, British Telecom research labs, data link and satellite earth stations to remote services and rural locations, cable laying and BT staff at work. The historical collection records the history of telecommunications from Alexander Graham Bell's first telephone, early cable ships and 19th Century telephone exchanges through to the present day.
Quantity*** Format S/M Colour C-D B/W

The Telegraph Colour Library Ltd
Unit C1, Enterprise Business Estate, Mastmaker Road, London E14 9TE
Tel: 071 987 1212
Contact: Colin James
Fax: 071 538 3309

General stock library now representing the Photo Source, including photography commissioned by the Telegraph Sunday Magazine. Wide range of subjects: agriculture, animals, commerce, fashion, food, health, industry, landscapes, military, personalities, people, sport, technology, transportation. Good general travel files - especially Australia, Canada, France, Germany, Hong Kong, Italy, UK, USA. Exclusive representation of **Space Frontiers** qv, Britain's most comprehensive collection of Space imagery. Free stock catalogue available on request.
Quantity**** Format S/M/L Colour D Illustration

Topham Picture Source
PO Box 33, Edenbridge, Kent TN8 5PB
Tel: 0342 850313
Contact: Alan Smith
Fax: 0342 850244
Telex: 95351 TOPHAM G

5,31, 76 Shoe Lane, London EC4R 3JB
Tel: 071 583 5900
Fax: 071 583 5901

One of the largest general agencies with colour and b/w pictures. Historic and up to date files. Convenient for Gatwick Airport and London. Our file of 5 million pictures includes personalities, pop, warfare, Royalty, sport, topography, France, natural history, plus a day by day world news file from original sources: **UPI (1932-70)** qv, INP, Press Association (1946-60), Central News (1903-36), Planet News (1932-), Alfieri (1914-40), Pictorial Press (1936-60). Agents for Associated Press Photos (APP) London, **Observer Colour Library** qv and Press Association Photos. Daily news update.
Quantity**** Format S Colour A-B-C-D B/W Illustration

B M Totterdell photography
Constable Cottage, Burlings Lane, Knockholt, Kent TN14 7PE
Tel: 0959 32001
Contact: B M Totterdell

Specialist volleyball library covering all aspects of the sport -
international, national, seniors, juniors, technical, coaching, referees,
personalities, tournaments, beach and recreational. The largest
collection in the UK.
Quantity Format S/M Colour D B/W**

Tessa Traeger
7 Rossetti Studios, 72 Flood Street, London SW3 5TF
Tel: 071 352 3641
Contact: Michelle Ingram

Food photographs in colour, 35mm and medium format including
many of a highly inventive nature. Gardens in England and France.
UK and foreign travel in colour on 35mm and general editorial
subjects including a selection of artists in colour and b/w. Visitors
welcome by appointment.
Quantity Format S/M Colour D B/W**

Tropix Photographic Library
156 Meols Parade, Meols, Wirral, Merseyside L47 6AN
Tel: 051 632 1698
Contact: Veronica Birley
Fax: 051 708 8733 [Attn Birley]

The developing world in all its aspects: environment and humankind.
Over 50,000 high quality images reflecting some 100 countries.
Extensive files from Africa, the Indian sub-continent, South East Asia,
Papua New Guinea, Central and South America, and growing
collections from the Middle and Far East. Specialist and well informed
pictures on the following subjects. Daily life: adults, children, crafts,
culture, education, housing, religions and many topics on medicine.
Economy: agriculture, aid, commerce, communications, industry,
irrigation, mining, refugees, technologies, trade, work. Environment:
conservation, desertification, alternative energy, erosion, landscapes,
land use, nature, pollution, recycling, salination and many aspects
of forests.
Quantity Format S/M Colour C-D B/W**

UK Pictures
32 Great Sutton Street, London EC1V 0DX
Tel: 071 608 2988
Contact: Duncan Raban
Fax: 071 250 3376

This is a London based picture and press agency with an expanding
library of over 200,000 colour transparencies and providing a daily
syndication service to 20 countries worldwide. Founded by sports
photographer Duncan Raban and originally called All-Action Picture
Library, it covers a varied range of personalities in all fields of show-
business, acting, pop music, politics and Royalty. UK Pictures also
specialises in world football as well as a wide variety of all major
sports and people at leisure. Commissions undertaken subject to
individual requirements.
Quantity* Format S Colour D B/W**

United Press International
UPI 1932 to 1970, PO Box 33, Edenbridge, Kent TN8 5PB
Tel: 0342 850313
Contact: Alan M Smith
Fax: 0342 850244
Telex: 95351 TOPHAM G

A major international newsfile commencing with Planet News in 1932
and incorporating International News Photos (INP). Approximately
one million negatives are filed with **Topham Picture Source** qv,
affording an unrivalled window on the past.
Quantity** B/W**

Universal Pictorial Press and Agency Ltd
30/34 New Bridge Street, London EC4V 6BN
Tel: 071 248 6730 [6 lines]
Contact: Terry Smith
Fax: 071 489 8982
Telex: 8952718 UNIPIX G

Syndication of a daily press and library service to national and
provincial press, periodicals, book publishers and TV. Over 400,000
colour transparencies on 35mm and medium format and 650,000
b/w negatives of international leaders and personalities, Royalty,
politics, civil service, trade unions, diplomats, law and order, military,
education, church, medical, business, literary, ballet, opera, orchestral,
associations, arts, stage, TV, films, pop, football, rugby, cricket, tennis,
golf, motor sports, equestrianism, boxing, wrestling, athletics,
swimming and skating, etc. Staff photographers available for press
and PR photography.
Quantity** Format S/M Colour B-C-D B/W**

USSR Photo Library
Conifers House, Cheapside Lane, Denham, Uxbridge,
Middlesex UB9 5AE
Tel: 0895 834814
Contact: Mark Wadlow
Fax: 0895 834028

A growing library on 35mm and medium format covering the Soviet
Union and specialising in subjects of tourist interest such as museums,
cathedrals, resorts, landmarks and people. Our main locations
include Baku, the Baltic Republics, Bukhara, Dushanbe, Kiev,
Leningrad, the Moldavian Republic, Moscow, Odessa, Samarkand,
Siberia, Sochi, Suzdal, Tashkent, Tbilisi, Vladimir, Yaroslavl and
Zagorsk. Local craftsmen, traditional and national costumes and
Russian dancing are also featured.
Quantity* Format S/M Colour D

V & A Picture Library
Victoria and Albert Museum, Cromwell Road, South Kensington,
London SW7 2RL
Tel: 071 938 8352/4
Contact: Isobel Sinden
Fax: 071 938 8353/8477
Telex: 268831 VICART G

A rapidly expanding, established picture library of 20,000 colour
transparencies, mostly medium format and quarter of a million b/w
images in the decorative and applied arts field. Wide range of
subjects with emphasis on ceramics, furniture, gold and silver, oriental
art, glass, jewellry, costume, textiles including carpets and tapestries,
ivories, enamels, stage and ballet, metalwork, prints and drawings,
Indian, Far Eastern and Islamic objects, musical instruments,
manuscripts, photographs, bookplates, sculpture, miniatures, toys
and dolls. B/W prints to order. Colour available immediately.
Express Service.
Quantity** Format S/M/L Colour A-B-C-D B/W**

The Venice Picture Library
2 St Peters Court, Porchester Road, London W2 5DR
Tel: 071 229 9808
Contact: Sarah Quill

A comprehensive photo library in colour and b/w covering most
aspects of the city of Venice, the islands and lagoon. The collection,
begun in 1970, is rapidly expanding. A list of subjects is available and
captions are accompanied by additional historical research if
required. Commissions undertaken and visitors are welcome by
appointment.
Quantity* Format S Colour C-D B/W

Viewfinder Colour Photo Library

The Production House, 147a St Michaels Hill, Cotham, Bristol BS2 8DB
Tel: 0272 237268
Contact: Sarah Boait
Fax: 0272 239198

Viewfinder is one of the fastest growing colour libraries in the UK. We are a general library and our continuously expanding files cover a wide range of subjects. We pride ourselves in our fast, efficient and friendly service. If you need pictures same day, we will get them to you by courier or Red Star - generally we dispatch by First Class Registered Mail. Call us today and find out how you can avoid search fees. Colour folder available.
Quantity* Format S/M/L Colour D**

The Vintage Magazine Co Ltd

203/213 Mare Street, London E8 3QE
Tel: 081 533 7588 ext 21
Contact: Marie Photiou
Fax: 081 533 3901

The complete picture supply service from one of the largest commercial archives in Europe. We have over 50,000 negatives covering movie stills, music, glamour and social history, 30,000 posters and newspapers from around the world, an uncountable collection of magazines filled with advertisements, pictures, artwork and cartoons, plus masses of sheet music, theatre bills, postcards, original photographs and printed ephemera of all kinds and periods. We are also the largest distributor of movie stills and posters in Europe.
Quantity** Format S/M/L Colour A-B-C-D B/W Illustration**

Visionbank Library Ltd

Riverside Studio B5, Metropolitan Wharf, Wapping Wall, London E1 9SS
Tel: 071 702 0023
Contact: Bruce Bailey
Fax: 071 480 7336

Many countries of the world and travel brochure subjects. Business, families, architecture, stately homes, agriculture, landscapes and many other subject categories suitable for a wide variety of uses. England Scene, our sister company, specialises in pictures of Britain and houses the largest collection of photographs of England, divided into regions and counties with a computerised cross-reference for ease of selection. Telephone for immediate service and same day dispatch.
Quantity** Format S/M/L Colour D Illustration**

Visnews Stills Library

Cumberland Avenue, Park Royal, London NW10 7EH
Tel: 081 453 4233/4227
Contact: Hanna Davies
Fax: 081 965 0620
Telex: 22678

A library of 35mm colour transparencies of international political leaders, personalities and locations. Videostills service available from Visnews' exclusive international coverage, BBC news material, client's own video cassette or Aston caption generator.
Quantity* Format S Colour C-D**

The Charles Walker Collection

Kingswood House, 180 Hunslet Road, Leeds, West Yorkshire LS10 1AF
Tel: 0532 433389
Contact: Jo Robinson
Fax: 0532 425605

This is one of the foremost collections in the world of subjects listed under the popular title of 'Mystery, Myth and Magic'. The library consists of over 12,000 colour transparencies and 5,000 b/w prints relating to arcane, esoteric, hermetic and occult subjects and is divided into eleven main sections. Alchemy, astral, astrology, demons, divination, herbal/medical, magical symbols, mystical sites, myths, practical occultism and witchcraft. Colour catalogue available on request.
Quantity Format M Colour D B/W Illustration**

John Walmsley Photo-Library

27 Wyeths Road, Epsom, Surrey KT17 4EB
Tel: 0372 743374
Contact: John Walmsley

Specialist collection of learning, training and working subjects. Schools, colleges, universities, adult education, skills centres, City Technology College, apprenticeship, etc. School section is catalogued by age and subject, including field trips, hobbies and sports. A growing collection of occupations. The collection reflects a multi-racial Britain. All material is recent, 35mm, in candid style with very natural interior lighting. Commissions undertaken. Most happy to discuss shooting on spec.
Quantity* Format S Colour D

Waterways Photo Library

39 Manor Court Road, Hanwell, London W7 3EJ
Tel: 081 840 1659
Contact: Derek Pratt

A specialist photo library on all aspect of Britain's inland waterways. Top quality 35mm and medium format colour transparencies, plus a large collection of b/w. Rivers and canals, bridges, locks, aqueducts, tunnels and waterside buildings, town and countryside scenes, waterway holidays, traditional canal art, boating, fishing and wildlife. Photographic commissions undertaken. Illustrated articles on waterway themes available. Also a growing collection of recent non-waterway material from England and Wales.
Quantity Format S/M Colour B-C-D B/W**

Weimar Archive

8-9 The Incline, Coalport, Telford, Shropshire TF8 7HR
Tel: 0952 680050
Contact: Dr Simon Taylor
Fax: 0952 587184

Picture library specialising in German and Central European history, politics and culture from the Middle Ages until 1945. Searches are computerised. Major categories include European Royalty; landscapes, architecture, people and culture in Europe pre-1914; illustrations of the First World War - photographs and paintings of all the major campaigns and the war at sea; an extensive collection of German painting, sculpture, literature, music, film and theatre, especially during the Weimar period and the Third Reich. Specialist material on anti-Semitism and the rise of Nazism. We cover science and technology, sport, travel, fashion and advertising and have recently added a collection on the German Democratic Republic. We also speak English!
Quantity Format S Colour A B/W Illustration**

West Air Photography

40 Alexandra Parade, Weston-Super-Mare, Avon BS23 1QZ
Tel: 0934 621333
Contact: Simon White
Fax: 0934 635421

Based at Weston-Super-Mare, the company operates commercial aircraft and operates all the year round. A growing library of more than 175,000 colour negatives, transparencies and b/w, cover locations all over England and South Wales. The photography satisfies a wide range of needs from advertising and promotions to planning applications, from civil engineering progress photography to geological surveys and applications such as infra-red photography for university research.
Quantity* Format M Colour C-D B/W**

Westcountry Pictures

23 Southernhay West, Exeter, Devon EX1 1PR
Tel: 0392 71937
Contact: Peter Cooper
Fax: 0392 50402 (ref Cooper)

Specialist library with mostly medium format colour transparencies of industries and places of interest in Devon and Cornwall. Subjects include traditional events, tourists, sports and marine events, modern and traditional architecture, villages and farms, all types of modern transport and communications, engineering, construction and farming industries, education, aerial and atmospheric landscapes and weather as well as local tourist attractions and leisure.
Quantity Format S/M/L Colour D B/W**

Eric Whitehead Picture Agency and Library
PO Box 33, Kendal, Cumbria LA9 4SU
Tel: 0539 733166/
0831 246264/0860 534767
Contact: Eric Whitehead

One of the world's largest libraries of snooker and indoor bowling photographs. Also a comprehensive collection of mountaineering, landscapes and heritage subjects. Major North of England events are covered for press and PR, TV stills and for magazines. Wire service available. Commissions undertaken.
Quantity** Format S Colour D B/W

Elizabeth Whiting & Associates
See **EWA Photo Library**

Janine Wiedel Photo Library
6 Stirling Road, Stockwell, London SW9 9EE
Tel: 071 737 0007
Contact: Janine Wiedel

A wide and continually expanding collection of social concern built up during twenty years of documentary reportage. An in-depth coverage of education, contemporary society, industry, women's issues including childbirth, ethnic groups, including Eskimos, Gypsies, Asian and Black communities in the UK and USA. Overseas coverage includes the Arctic, Iceland, Galapagos Islands, Iran, Europe and USA. Commissions undertaken. Clients welcome by appointment. Leaflet available.
Quantity*** Format S Colour C-D B/W

Wiener Library Ltd
4 Devonshire Street, London W1N 2BH
Tel: 071 636 7247
Contact: Alexandra Wiessler
Fax: 071 436 6428

This is a private library funded by charitable donations. The collection includes material on the Holocaust, Germany before, during and after World War Two, Jewish history and life, refugees and migration, war activities and war crimes and trials and all allied subjects. The collection also includes cartoons, posters and leaflets, photo albums and many identity cards, certificates and examples of forms and questionnaires.
Quantity** B/W Illustration

Wilderness Photographic Library
2 Kent View, Waterside, Kendal, Cumbria LA9 4HE
Tel: 0539 728334
Contact: John Noble
Fax: 05396 21293

An expanding 35mm colour library specialising in mountain and wilderness regions worldwide, including associated aspects of people, places, natural history, geographical features, exploration, mountaineering and adventure sports. Material is suitable for advertising, publishing, postcards, calendars, TV and film location. Assignments undertaken.
Quantity* Format S Colour B-C-D

Andy Williams Photo-Library
3 Levylsdene, Merrow, Guildford, Surrey GU1 2RS
Tel: 0483 572778
Contact: Andy Williams

A comprehensive coverage on medium and large format of the British Isles and near continent. Specialist landscape and architectural collection includes London, castles, historic houses, great gardens, cottages, golfing scenes, country scenes, moods of nature, waterfalls, windmills, lighthouses, etc. Library visits welcome and commissions readily undertaken.
Quantity** Format M/L Colour C-D

David Williams Picture Library
50 Burlington Avenue, Kelvindale, Glasgow G12 0LH
Tel: 041 339 7823
Contact: David Williams

A personal collection of 35mm and medium format colour transparencies of Scotland and of Iceland. The main topics covered are landscapes, countryside scenes, historic sites, geology and geomorphology.
Quantity** Format S/M Colour D

S & I Williams Power Pix International Picture Library
Castle Lodge, Wenvoe, Cardiff CF5 6AD
Tel: 0222 595163
Contact: Steven Williams
Fax: 0222 593905

Comprehensive and expanding colour library on all formats. A wide range of subjects includes abstracts, agriculture, aviation, ballooning, birds, boats, butterflies, castles, children, churches, clouds, couples, diving, fish and fishing, flowers, fungi, gardens, girls and glamour, industry, landscapes, lightning, mountaineering, natural history, people worldwide, sunsets, sport, sub-aqua, transport, trees, watersports and yachting. Countries covered include especially America, Australia, Canada, Europe, India, Japan and Britain. Commissions undertaken. Colour posters and catalogue available on request.
Quantity*** Format S/M/L Colour A-B-C-D

The Wingfield Sporting Art Library
35 Sibella Road, London SW4 6JA
Tel: 071 622 6301
Contact: Mary Ann Wingfield
Fax: 071 622 6301

The Wingfield Sporting Library is a unique colour and b/w library specialising in sporting works of art, both historical and contemporary. The library was formed to reproduce high quality, large format colour transparencies of paintings and some prints, covering 50 different sports. It was originally inspired by Mary Ann Wingfield's *Sport and the Artist* series of books published by the Antique Collectors Club which trace the history and the art of each sport. Research commissions welcome. Clients by appointment.
Quantity* Format S/M Colour D B/W Illustration

Roger Wood
45 Victoria Road, Deal, Kent CT14 7AY
Tel: 0304 372786
Contact: Roger Wood
Fax: c/o 0304 365766
Telex: 477719 A/B MARFIL
attn Roger Wood

A specialist library concentrating mainly on countries in the Middle East, with particular reference to tourism and antiquities. Includes Egypt, all the North African countries, Iran, some Gulf states, Greece, Turkey and Ethiopia. Also Pakistan and Bangladesh. Colour is mostly medium format. Many items available in b/w.
Quantity** Format M Colour B-C-D B/W

Woodmansterne Picture Library
2 Greenhill Crescent, Watford Business Park, Watford, Hertfordshire WD1 8RD
Tel: 0923 228236
Contact: Johanna
Fax: 0923 245788

Britain, Europe and the Holy Land. Architecture, especially cathedrals and stately home interiors, painting, sculpture, decorative arts, interior design, natural history, butterflies, geography, volcanos, transport, space exploration, opera and ballet, seasonal and sunset views, major state occasions. All in colour.
Quantity** Format S/M/L Colour A-B-C-D

Michael Woodward Licensing

Parlington Hall, Parlington, Aberford, West Yorkshire LS25 3EG
Tel: 0532 813913
Contact: Michael Woodward
Fax: 0532 813911
Telex: 55293 CHACOM G

International art licencing agents for art and photography, representing over 100 illustrators, artists and photographers. Specialists in design for greeting cards, stationery, calendars, fine art prints, posters and jigsaws. Besides producing commissioned artwork, we have extensive files on most subjects available on large format transparencies through our art library. Brochure available on request. Offices in Antwerp and New York.
Quantity Format L Colour D Illustration**

World Pictures

1st Floor, 85a Great Portland Street, London W1N 5RA
Tel: 071 437 2121 / 436 0440
Contact: Gerry Brenes
Fax: 071 439 1307

Specialised collection aimed at the travel and holiday market. Over 300,000 transparencies in medium format, showing countries, cities and resorts throughout the world, likely to interest tour operators and others producing brochures. Files also include a wide selection of 'emotive' holiday material suitable for cover and display use. Coverage of popular resort areas updated annually. Photographers available for assignment.
Quantity** Format M / L Colour D**

World Press Network Ltd

112 Westbourne Park Road, London W2 5PL
Tel: 071 221 5587
Contact: Sonja Neraas
Fax: 071 792 2181
Telex: 94012781 WPNL G

Specialised researches for beauty, fashion, relationships, food, home and family features, in colour and b/w. Text supplied on all types of topics - news, sport, personalities, business, politics - particularly Australian politicians - health and diet, fiction, homes and gardens, Australian celebrities and personalities. Celebrity interviews from freelancers with offices in New York and Australia provide a fast and efficient service in carrying out requests for material not at hand. Syndication includes Marie Claire Group, *Golf Monthly,* Australian Consolidated Press, Fairfax Newspaper Group, IPC monthlies, IPC Holborn Group, *Follow Me, Femina, What Diet* and *Lifestyle* and numerous freelance journalists all over the world.
Quantity Format S / M / L Colour D B/W Illustration**

George Wright

Mountover Farm, Rampisham, Dorchester, Dorset DT2 0PL
Tel: 0935 83333
Contact: George Wright

Photographers' own collection including English and European gardens, landscape, people, events and cookery as featured in the pages of the *Observer, Telegraph* and *Independent* magazines. Co-author of *English Topiary Gardens* (Weidenfeld & Nicholson). Some coverage of the Middle East, India and Nepal.
Quantity Format S / M Colour C-D**

York Archaeological Trust for Excavation and Research Ltd

1 Pavement, York, North Yorkshire YO1 2NA
Tel: 0904 643211 ext 223
Contact: Keith M Buck
Fax: 0904 640029

The authoritative archive of the antiquities, archaeology and architecture of the City of York and surrounding areas. The library holds in excess of 40,000 colour transparencies and as many b/w negatives, illustating the heritage of this ancient and attractive city. Original photography of the city and surrounding areas, archaeological excavations, archaeologists and their techniques, and superlative images of their finds, with magnificent details of many artefacts, all represent the finest aspects of modern archaeological science. The presentation of archaeology, architecture and the city's heritage to the public is also extensively covered, including photographs of the world famous Jorvik Viking Centre.
Quantity* Format S / M / L Colour C-D B/W**

The John Robert Young Collection

61 De Montfort Road, Lewes, East Sussex BN7 1SS
Tel: 0273 475216
Contact: Jennifer Barrett

This is a distinctive picture collection of fine images, including historical material, on the French Foreign Legion, the People's Liberation Army (China), The Spanish Legion and the Royal Marines. Also a multitude of transparencies from all parts of the globe on varying subjects - water pollution in Colombia, natural childbirth (Dr Michael Odent), Texas Rangers, Britain's choir schools and an ever increasing collection on women priests and other religious subjects. The library also contains scenic material from Britain, France, Djibouti, Corsica, Hong Kong, Malta, Morocco, French Guyane including Devil's Island, etc. A small b/w collection includes 'Swinging 60's', Thames lightermen, premature childbirth, rodeo's, Hong Kong boat people and Brighton. All material is of the highest quality being shot with Leitz lenses.
Quantity Format S Colour C-D B/W**

FOREIGN MEMBERS

Alok Productions

c/o BAPLA, 13 Woodberry Cresent, London N10 1PJ
Tel: 081 444 7913
Fax: 081 883 9215

Extensive collection in colour, b/w, all formats, specialising in the ancient civilisations of Asia Minor and the landscape of Anatolia. The collection covers 20,000 years of historical, archaeological, architectural, social religious, decorative and industrial fabric of the past inhabitants of the area. Mausoleums, castles, palaces, temples, rock drawings, churches, mosques and houses. Mountains, lakes, rivers and seashores. Arabian and North African deserts. Underwater photography, especially the Red Sea.
Quantity** Format S / M / L Colour C-D B/W**

Maxwell's Photo Agency

Dargle House, 98 Lower Drumcondra Road, Dublin 9 EIRE
Tel: 0001 308072
Contact: Marie Maxwell
Fax: 0001 307237

Our agency has been in business in Dublin since 1955. We have a large range of pictures covering Irish life style, political happenings and personalities who made the news from this period up to the present time. Irish literary Greats and artists are on file including a unique collection of Brendan Behan. Irish working life such as basket making, cheese making, harps and many other subjects are available in b/w and colour along with all the news-making pictures taken since we started. Wire photo transmitting machines, b/w and colour in use.
Quantity* Format S / M Colour B-C-D B/W**

The Slide File

79 Merrion Square, Dublin 2, EIRE
Tel: 0001 766850 / 686086
Contact: George Munday
Fax: 0001 608332

Just 100 yards from the Dail - the Irish Parliament - The Slide File is situated in the finest Georgian square in the British Isles. The company was set up in 1979 by two professional photographers and has since become the authoritative source for Irish pictures. The images have been widely used by publishers of books and magazines and for advertising campaigns in the UK, the USA and Europe. Fifty photographers regularly supplement the 30,000 carefully edited transparencies which, apart from a small international section, illustrate most aspects of Irish Life.
Quantity Format S / M / L Colour C-D**

FOREIGN MEMBERS CONTINUED

The Stock House Ltd
Room 1202 On Hong, Commercial Bldg, 141-147 Hennessy Road,
Wanchai, HONG KONG
Tel: 0108525 8660887
Contact: Ivy Davis
Fax: 0108525 8662212

A general library containing over 350,000 colour transparencies on
all formats, covering all parts of the globe, with a major collection of
Asian material. Affiliated to libraries in London, New York and Tokyo.
Stock pictures for advertising and editorial from around the world.
Quantity**** Format S/M/L Colour C-D

NEW MEMBERS

Cable and Wireless Visual Resource
Corporate Affairs
Cable and Wireless
New Mercury House, 26 Red Lion Square, London WC1R 4UQ
Tel: 071 315 4885
Fax: 071 315 5052
Contact: Lesley A Wood

Cable and Wireless plc is one of the world's leading international
telecommunications groups with business in some 50 countries. In
support of our activities, slides are made of local scenes, cityscapes
and general views as well as technical material such as
telecommunications equipment, earth stations and cable ships. Our
scope includes the Caribbean, Far East and the USA. Images are
produced to a level suitable for corporate literature and display
purposes. Joint photographic assignments may be considered.
Enquiries can be taken by post, phone or personal visits by
appointment.

Country Life Library
Kings Reach Tower, Stamford Street, London SE1 9LS
Tel: 071 261 6337
Fax: 071 261 5139
Contact: Camilla Costello

A unique collection of photographs of exceptional quality, mainly
black and white, dating back to 1897, of country houses, churches and
houses in Britain and abroad. Interiors showing architectural details
of ceilings, fireplaces, furniture, paintings and sculpture. Exteriors
showing many fine landscaped gardens, including those by Gertrude
Jekyll. The Library is open Tuesdays and Thursdays from 10.00am to
5.00pm. Visits by appointment only.

Director Picture Library
Mountbarrow House, Elizabeth Street, London SW1W 9RB
Tel: 071 730 6060
Fax: 071 235 5627
BAPLA representative Ruth Williamson

Director Picture Library is a newly established photo libray
specialising in business and political portraiture. the subjects are
drawn principally from articles and company profiles featured in
Director magazine, where a wide selection of specially commissioned
pictures has been assembled. The nature of the source means that the
library is constantly expanding. Prominent politicians of all
persuasions include Neil Kinnock, Tony Benn, Cecil Parkinson;
business figures such as Lords Young, King and Weinstock, less
categorised figures; Cardinal Hume, Dr Runcie and the Duke of
Westminster are all available from a file of mono and colour
transparencies.

Ecoscene
4 Heatherview Cottages, Shortfield, Frensham, Surrey GU10 3BH
Tel: 025125 4395
BAPLA representative Sally Morgan

Colour coverage of all aspects of natural history with particular
emphasis on the effects of man on the environment throughout the
world. Main subject areas include acid rain, animals, birds,
conservation, earth sciences, energy, flowers, fungi, global warming,
habitats, habitat loss, industry, insects, mammals, plants, pollution (all
forms), rainforests, recycling, rubbish, trees and urban wildlife. The
library is run by a professional ecologist who has expert knowlege of
environmental issues and can provide a comprehensive service to the
picture researcher. Commissions are undertaken. A detailed subject
index is available on request.

Images of Africa Photo Bank
11 The Windings, Lichfield, Staffordshire WS13 7EX
Tel: 0543 262898
Fax: 0543 417154
BAPLA representative David Keith Jones

60,000 transparencies and 50,000 b/w negatives of Africa. Kenya is
covered in great detail. Excellent material on Botswana, Egypt,
Rwanda, Tanzania, Uganda, Zaire, Zambia and Zimbabwe. The
natural beauty, tourism attractions, landscapes, birds, animals, forests,
mountains, lakes, coast, people, cities and towns of the region.
Especially strong sections on African wildlife, National Parks and
Reserves, people and their way of life. Assignments undertaken.

The Raymond Mander and Joe Mitchenson
Theatre Collection
The Mansion, Beckenham Place Park, Beckenham, Kent BR3 2BP
Tel: 081 658 7725
BAPLA representative

The Mander and Mitchenson collection can supply pictures of all
aspects of British Theatre from its earliest days. Our files include
theatres, plays, musicals, opera, ballet, pantomine, music hall and
circus; we also have files on actors, singers, dancers, composers,
conductors, musicians, dramatists, directors and designers. We have
posters, programmes, paintings, engravings, set and costume designs,
books, magazines and artefacts. We supply pictures to book,
magazine and newspaper publishers, to film and TV companies,
interior designers and academics. We have access to individuals with
specific expertise as consultants. We also answer questions.

Stock Shot
Mirefoot, Burneside, Kendal, Cumbria LA8 9AB
Tel: 0539 740770
Fax: 0539 731546
BAPLA representative Jess Stock

The Stock Shot library contains solely the work of Jess Stock, ex-British
ski champion, ex-mountaineer and ex Yeti-hunter with Chris
Bonnington and BBC2. Primarily skiing shots, mountaineering,
mountain biking and expeditions, the latter in Pakistan, Nepal, Tibet
and New Zealand. Office and library are based in Cumbria but the
winter months are spent in the French Alps, producing action ski
photography with the latest equipment and fashions, tourist shots and
plenty with children. Many images feature the British Ski Team since
Jess is their official photographer.

Sylvia Cordaiy Photo Library
77 East Ham Road, Littlehampton, West Sussex BN1 BU
Tel: 0903 715297
Fax: 0903 726318
Contact: Sylvia Cordaiy

This fast growing library holds comprehensive files on the following
subjects: Architecture and travel worldwide; Global environmental
topics; The archive of Paul Kaye (specialising in animals and people)
contributor to Picture Post and Reveille; UK counties, landscapes,
cities, villages etc; Teh RSPCA at work with wild and domestic animals;
The Pony Drift; People at play; The Tall Ships and Yachting; Large
selection of images related to the card and calendar market.
Photographers available for commissions. Clients and picture
researchers welcome.

★ ELFANDE

PUBLISHERS & PROMOTERS OF
CREATIVE PEOPLE AROUND
THE GLOBE!